A
ROUND
of
GOLF
with
TOMMY
ARMOUR

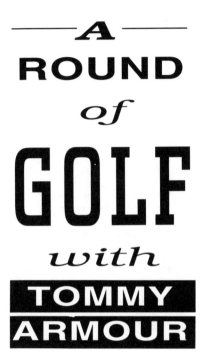

A
ROUND
of
GOLF
with
TOMMY
ARMOUR

L&B

LYONS & BURFORD, PUBLISHERS

This book is dedicated to a million hopefuls like my pal Bill

Design by Catherine Lau Hunt
Illustrations by Manuel F. Cheo

Printed in the United States of America
10 9 8 7 6 5 4 3

Library of Congress Cataloging-in-Publication Data

Armour, Tommy.
   A round of golf with Tommy Armour / by Tommy Armour.
     p. cm.
   ISBN 1-55821-217-5
    1. Golf. I. Title.
   GV965.A75 1993   *92-39124*
   796.352—dc20   *CIP*

Contents

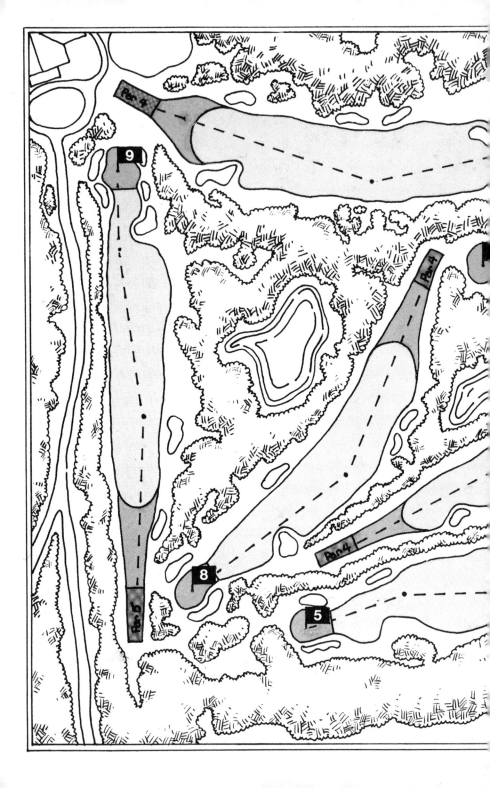

The Scene of *A Round of Golf*

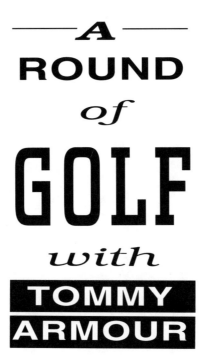

A
ROUND
of
GOLF
with
TOMMY
ARMOUR

*T*his is a true story.

Or so nearly true that you won't know the difference. So much of the story has happened to you that you may think you are one of the golfers I'm telling about. You may be.

I have been in this story or some variation of it many times. That is the reason it is being put into type instead of being limited to the view and hearing of other fellows I've played and taught, as it has been previously.

At our club there is a man named Bill. In some ways he is enough like you to be you.

I don't think I knew what his handicap was when this story began. I'd seen him out on the course sometimes making a shot that looked very good. A few other times I'd watch him on another fairway hitting the ball so poorly that in simple sporting decency I pretended I hadn't seen him.

Our friend Bill was strictly a golfer of the people. He played about as 85 per cent of golfers do; he was needlessly bad on about a third of his shots and only moderately good the rest of the time.

One day I had a game arranged with three other fellows and while two of them and I were sitting in the grillroom shortly after noon one of them telephoned that he wasn't going to be able to play. He said he had been forced to devote himself to hard labor in the city.

I walked out to the locker room to get into my golf shoes and there was Bill taking shirts, slacks, shoes and other belongings out of his locker and packing them into a bag.

"Leaving town?" I asked.

"No," he grunted.

"Got a game?"

He shook his head and continued to clear out his locker.

"Well, come on with us. Mac had to back out and you can fill in with Ed and Jim and me."

"Nope." Bill was emphatic. "I'm quitting golf."

I laughed and suggested, "Why not quit after playing eighteen more?"

He glared at me and stuffed another shirt into his luggage as he related his sad story.

"Tommy, I'm not fooling. I'm absolutely through. There's no sense or fun playing like I did yesterday. I'm ashamed of the stinking, horrible imitation of golf I've been playing lately. I refuse to punish myself one more round." With that woeful declaration Bill snapped the lock on his bag.

"Too bad," I said. "You are a nice guy and you ought to be enjoying the companionship of other pleasant fellows out here. But if you've made up your mind some of the boys are going to miss taking your money."

"That, of course, will break my heart," Bill murmured.

"And you won't be getting the two or three dollars you always take on those Nassaus from your clumsy chum, Jerry," I reminded him.

"There is one man I can beat," Bill reflected and brightened a bit.

"And you will miss the money from that poor hopeless hacker, Burton. You ought to be arrested for not giving him more strokes. You are quitting with him on your conscience."

"He just has bad luck on a lot of shots," Bill told me.

"Maybe so," I conceded. "But forget him. Do you know why you are a much worse golfer than you've got any reason for being, and why you're discouraged and a quitter?"

Bill began to burn a bit. That amused me. I have talked frankly, even almost insultingly, in getting fellows jarred into playing good golf. Bill was like the rest of them; he couldn't be coddled into learning a first-class game.

He looked through a locker-room window and saw pals of his on the beautiful green course. Then he turned to me and asked, "What's wrong with me and my golf?"

"You are practically brainless when you get a golf club in your hands. That's all."

I let that bore in, then continued: "I don't know where your head goes when you walk up to a golf shot -- the same head that has made you a big success in business. On a golf course you are a bum a lot of the time entirely because you can't or won't think."

"And you are a mental marvel, one of golf's greatest eggheads?" Bill asked sourly.

I admitted that others have argued that with me. "But let me tell you, my fretful friend, with my brains and even that spotty swing of yours, your golf would be so much better it would be a different game. The sun would be shining, the birds would be singing, the fellows you'd be playing against would be moaning and paying you, and all would be well with the world."

Bill began opening his bag.

After a few more conversational waggles while Bill was putting on his golf clothes and shoes, we went out to the first tee to join Ed and Jim.

*T*he first tee at our club is about like that at any other good club on a pleasant afternoon.

Some fellows are making stiff and jerky chops instead of swinging at the ball to get the round started. They're topping, pushing their drives off to the right or smothering hooks. The competent ones allow the club to hit the ball.

Several are carelessly and loosely taking practice swings and endangering life and limb of other golfers and caddies who are sleepwalking in the first tee area. When their turn comes to step up to hit their drives they invariably tighten up and get stiff in the muscles and soft in the head.

There are three or four on the practice putting green near the first tee. They are grimly working on 10- to 25-foot putts that they hole now and then due to a combination of 60 per cent luck and 40 per cent (or less) skill. The 2- to 4-foot putts that are the critical ones, and that depend 98 per cent on skill, are not being practiced.

Apparently everybody expects the opposition to concede those short putts that are so easily and frequently missed after the opponent looks the other way instead of saying "that's good."

The reclaimed runaway, Bill, and Ed and Jim and I come onto the tee talking about who gets how many strokes and who will be partners and what the team and individual bets will be. That's the usual script everywhere. Regardless of the handicapping systems there'll always be debates about handicaps.

The higher mathematics and applied psychology of the handicapping systems are offered to balance competition and to protect gentlemen sportsmen and ladies against the calculated sins of competitors. But rarely are these devices accepted without question by contenders who are arranging matches on the first tee. The pleading and the bargaining are part of the fun with many golfers.

And, when golf associations themselves can't agree on handicap systems, the golfers can't be expected to accept without question any handicap proposal made to them.

Bill and I were teamed by the deal we had made in the locker room. Our opponents, naturally, wanted me to give them too many strokes and didn't want to give Bill enough. Eventually we decided to play the sides even, with me thinking the shots for my partner and playing my own game, too.

The few dollars involved didn't mean money to any of us but we are the sort of competitors who enjoy talking about something more than a moral victory when we are at the 19th hole and reviewing the battle.

While we were engaged in the traditional rites of matchmaking at the first tee I made an apparently casual examination of Bill's clubs. I've seen many instances of golfers being badly handicapped by ill-fitting equipment. When I hear laments about bad play I look at the mourner's tools and often I wonder how the fellow or girl can get a decent shot once out of three tries, considering the clubs being used.

When you realize that a golf club positions the player's hands 40 inches, more or less, from a ball 1.68 inches in diameter that must be hit precisely after a swing that may take the clubhead on a round trip of as much as 26 or 27 feet, you become aware of the importance of using clubs conforming correctly to your requirements.

Bill's clubs were adequate, better fitting than the clubs of most middle-aged men, who try to use clubs that are too heavy, with shafts that are too stiff. He had a driver and numbers 1, 3, 4 and 5 woods. His driver had, I'd guess, a little more than eleven degrees of loft and that's as it should be. The shafts were a bit supple and they helped him get the whip that most golf shafts should have.

Fortunately, then, the first of Bill's three problems was solved. He had the right clubs. The next two questions were, did he know when and how to use them? Any golfer who scores 80 or higher throws away strokes by incorrect choice of clubs.

As I completed my hasty inspection of my partner's equipment he flipped a coin to determine who had the honor.

The enemy won the toss. Jim stepped up and teed his ball. He is a fellow who never let himself get out of condition after he left college sports. He moves gracefully. He's got fine co-ordination. He is a great hunter. He is a good natural golfer. He'd be better if he used his head more, but against most of his competition he doesn't have to play brainy golf. He whipped the club easily at the ball and drove about 220 down the middle. His partner was one of the famous college and pro football tackles. He is strong enough to flatten the ball but the ball doesn't know it. He messes up too many of his shots with a violent waste of energy. He grabbed his club with a crushing grip, swung strenuously and duck-hooked his drive into the rough about 150 yards out. He could have done better swinging easy with a 5-iron.

Ed was still bent over to pick up his wooden peg when my man hurried up to tee his ball.

"Half a minute, Billy," I called to him. "Here is where my brain begins working for you. Why your rush? You're not ready to hit."

"What's the matter? You want to drive first?" Bill asked.

"No, I want you to start slowing down and smoothing out your swing before it starts. The ball will wait for you. Take another club or two out of your bag and swing them together the way a baseball player does when he is waiting his turn at bat."

Ty Cobb was the one who is responsible for that idea. The old baseball star had a 24-year batting average of .367, which was 25 points higher than Ruth's 22-year average. So you've got to admit Ty knew a bit about hitting a ball. He was the first ballplayer to swing two or three bats before he stepped up to the plate.

Ty became an enthusiastic golfer, and we've had many talks on techniques in golf and baseball. He told me that swinging the several bats helped him get loosened and stretched, developed his hand action, made it easier for him to have a feeling of certain control of the bat when he was swinging at pitching, and instinctively conditioned him for moving in good balance.

I adapted Ty's idea to my own preliminaries at the first tee and recommended it to my pupils, for whom it did considerably more good than what they thought were "practice" swings.

Swinging those clubs gave Bill a little warm-up and subconsciously put some rhythm into his swing. He had been going at the job like most ordinary golfers at the first tee, impatient to snatch the club away from the ball and get the ball moving by lunging and chopping at it, instead of by swinging and hitting.

The golfer who is nervous at the first tee needn't think that he differs from a lot of the experts. The nervous experts, however, think of something they've got to do to make sure of hitting a good shot. They do that instead of letting the mind go blank or freezing in panic.

It's natural for an intelligent and imaginative golfer to be apprehensive at the first tee. He doesn't know what's ahead in eighteen holes. He probably hasn't been playing for several days — maybe a week or more — and isn't sure of his swing.

I've known only one quite intelligent man who was sublimely confident at the first tee. We were at Boca Raton and as we were arranging the match, instead of reciting the customary alibis and dismal stories of recent past performance, he blithely remarked, "I've never been playing better in my life than I have been lately."

The rest of us almost fainted from shock.

Another case I recall is that of a young professional making his debut in championsbip golf who provided the most pitiable exhibition of nerves I've seen. It was in a qualifying round of a British Open championship. The lad hit the first drive about fifteen feet. He made the out nine in 51 with a deuce on the most difficult hole at Carnoustie.

Later he told me that the sight of the gallery frightened him so he could hardly move. The only gallery he'd had prior to his first round in the Open was his caddie, the men with whom he happened to be playing at the club where he worked, and their caddies.

Happily, I am blessed with a temperament that has made me immune to the first-tee version of stage fright but I am sympathetically aware of the shaky state of those who do suffer from it. So I tried to get Bill feeling at ease and confident and forgetting the other fellows.

"Tee the ball high enough so the clubface will meet it in the middle on the upswing. You've got to trust your swing now. Hit the ball with a purpose instead of a foggy hope."

Bill smiled wanly.

"What can you possibly have to worry about?" I asked him. "I am the guy to worry if there is any worrying to be done. You are playing this round with my reputation and your swing. I would like to have you concentrate on how you are going to hit the ball rather than where you're going to hit it."

"O.K., send me in, Coach," my partner responded. He walked to the left side of the tee, pressed his peg into the turf and placed his ball for the drive.

"Hold it!" I called to him. He stepped away from the ball.

"What's wrong?" he asked.

"You're not making use of my brains." I looked at Ed and Jim and asked, "Do you fellows mind? There's nobody waiting and pushing to follow us and I want to do the right thing by

Bill. It'll take us some time. Do you want to go along or call our game off?"

"Go ahead; I may get something good besides your money out of this afternoon," Ed remarked. Jim nodded.

Then I said to my partner and pupil, "I want to show you something that not three out of a hundred fairly good golfers know about playing smart and safe golf. Pick up your tee and your ball."

3 YOU PLAY A GOLF COURSE, TOO (The First Hole)

*B*ill had made the commonest mistake in golf. He knew he was playing golf but he forgot he was playing a golf course.

Comparatively few golfers ever show they are aware that the golf architect tries to design a course that rewards an intelligent golfer and penalizes a stupid one.

In fact, I sometimes wonder if the majority of golfers are even aware that there is such an art as that of the competent golf architect's.

When I told Bill that he was to concentrate on hitting the ball with a purpose I gave him credit for appreciating that the purpose was to hit the ball to where the next shot would be easy. You would think that foresight would be almost instinctive, but the simple job of charting the course wisely in a round of golf is something that not many have mastered. You may recall that the latest round you played was marred by strokes lost because you didn't use your brains in solving the most obvious and easiest problems the golf architect could present.

The first hole at our course is a long par 4. It is about 430 yards from the middle of the tee to the middle of the green. The markers seldom are forward on the tee. The hole is a dogleg to the left. There are traps on the left out about 200 to 250 yards. On the left, too, is fairly heavy rough. The fairway is reasonably wide.

You can see from the diagram of our first hole that there shouldn't be any architectural problems to give an average golfer like Bill a bad start. A drive of 200 yards or so would put him in good position to make the dogleg and have a second shot with plenty of fairway.

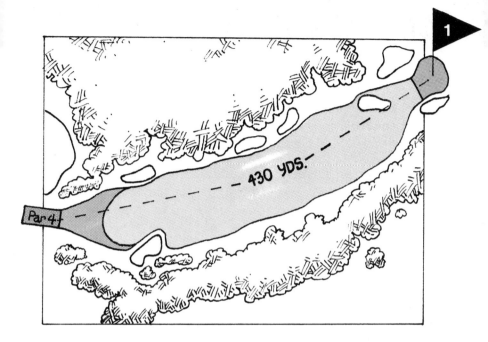

The average golfer will have to get his third shot close enough to the hole to get down in one putt if he is going to get pars on any of the par-4 holes that are 370 yards or over.

When Bill had teed his ball on the left side of the first tee he hadn't used his brains and I told him so.

"Your first move has been thoughtless. Now let me show you how a golfer uses his head," I said.

"I haven't made a move," Bill protested.

"Yes, you did. You teed the ball where a hook would get you into the rough. Now tee your ball on the right side of the tee. You see that the fairway goes out to the right so you've got leeway in case you slice and plenty of room in case you hook. You want to hit your drive out into space. The more space you've got, the more room you allow yourself as a margin for error, the more relaxed your swing will be," I explained.

"That makes sense," my partner admitted. "I should have

learned that when Ed teed up just about where I did and hooked into the rough."

"Get in the habit of visualizing your objective, figuring out your strategy so that even if you don't hit your shot well you won't be in trouble. You've got to be thinking that there are wise places and stupid and dangerous places for you to have your ball on every one on the eighteen tees. If you tee your ball thoughtlessly on all, or most, of the eighteen tees, you are liable to produce a horrifying addition to your score."

TRAP–
230 YDS.
TO GREEN

BILL'S DR

CROSS TRAP—
75 YDS
TO GREEN

BILL'S ATTEMPTED SECOND SHOT (actually fell short into trap)

SHOT ADVISED BY ARMOUR

430 YDS.

BUSH—
150 YDS.
TO GREEN

"I never thought of it that way," Bill confessed. "I'll take that as a lesson that I can use," said Jim. "I'd not paid any attention to that part of the game."

"No, but you always were canny in figuring out how to play for batters and pitchers when you were playing baseball. You played smart when you were punting and the other team had a safety man who might run the ball back 75 yards on you. But as a good athlete it doesn't seem to have occurred to you that you also have to play smart ball when your opponent is the golf course," I reminded Jim.

There were several other points I wanted to bring out to get my partner realizing that almost everything he did on a golf course gave him a chance to make valuable use of his brains.

"You've never figured out your own course. This is the first time in all the years you've belonged here that you ever have had suggested to you that you might be thinking about the best way for you to get around the course," I told Bill.

The remark also applied to our opponents. Maybe Jim, due entirely to his athletic instinct, had studied the course a little more than the average golfer does, but the other two fellows had looked at the course hundreds of times and had seen very little. They couldn't have told you how far away from tees key traps are located, how long the traps extend, the distance from the center of the green of distinctive trees or other landmarks, how far away from tee or green and how wide ditches or ponds are, or how much distance they could get consistently from their respective clubs.

The golfer as a youngster engages in a number of games played on standard sizes of playing fields. Football, baseball, basketball, tennis and many other sports lack the intriguing and educational element that golf has in its course architecture. But there is no standard golf course. Hence the golfer often has a feeling of being baffled or unlucky when a shot finishes in trouble that he hadn't anticipated.

As I reflected on my partner's complete unawareness that he could help himself play better golf by using foresight in teeing his ball for his drive, I realized that by using some course-sense in his game Bill not only was going to improve his golf but enjoy it more.

There is a thrill in hitting a fine shot. There is an equally pleasant thrill in intelligently maneuvering the ball around the course with the definite idea of getting from point to point with the least risk and in the fewest strokes.

The best course architecture is an imitation of nature. The prime exhibit of this imitation is the Old Course at St. Andrews. This course is still the classic upon which fundamental tactics of play are based. There have been some changes made in refining the crude nature of the Old Course since it was established on the treeless lean pasture bordering the North Sea. However, the principles of design are unchanged.

Where the clubs of pioneer golfers shoveled out the sandy soil, and relentless winds combined and enlarged those early divots into traps, you now see significant bunkering that has retained the course's value despite the immense changes in the ball and the clubs. What howls there would be now on modern courses if bunkers were placed where the most shots land! In a mistaken effort to eliminate interesting, testing problems that add to golf's charm, rough has been reduced, in many instances, to such dull and innocuous status that Whistler's Mother could play out of it without losing a stroke. Distances from tees and greens have been marked by stakes, signs or alien-appearing shrubs in eliminating another factor to test the player's judgment. As a result, many golfers never appreciate what pleasant excitement there can be to thinking of and beating the course. They never learn to play with the course, too.

When you play golf you are playing a game with precision instruments. One ounce of pressure lacking in your shot, a few degrees' deviation from the required plane in the angle of the clubface, a swift, spasmodic swing, a lift of your head — and you come up empty on the shot. You don't want to add to the odds against you by forgetting that the course might trap and ruin what you believed, without thinking, was a good shot.

Golf is a game of percentages. The expert knows the greater percentage of shots will come off. The player who scores 85 or higher doesn't have that confidence in the odds favoring him. That absence of confidence has a subconscious effect in making his shots tougher.

The ordinary golfer shouldn't be discouraged if he doesn't make fast progress in learning to read the course and to govern himself accordingly. He discovers that it takes some experience to discipline himself so he deliberately shoots short and for strategic position, instead of taking a chance on pulling off a perfect shot.

One of the finest shotmakers in professional golf has fallen short of achieving a magnificent record of top championships simply because courses tempted him to take unwise chances. When his shots were not perfectly executed he often found himself in dire distress.

I was paired with him when early in a championship he made one little mistake of muscle, pushing his drive out into the rough. The hole was a par 5 with a stream wandering to the left and well in front of the green. Then came the sad failure to play the course. He took a wood when he was about 300 yards from the green and knocked the ball into the water to the left. His 7 on that hole shook him. He never quite got well but did finish high in a championship he might have won by playing the course with a high order of golf intelligence.

His mental error was exactly the same as that of the 100-shooter who is in the rough farther away from the green than he possibly can make in one shot, yet tries to get distance out of the rough. He doesn't execute the shot perfectly, and is in worse position than he was before attempting the recovery, with one more stroke on his card.

The simple, logical policy in such cases is to play two easy shots; one easy recovery shot and the next an easy shot to the green. About 75 per cent of these situations find the thoughtless golfer playing three or four exceedingly dangerous shots instead of the two safe ones.

Why? Because he doesn't use even the minimum amount of brains.

After Bill had teed his ball at the correct place and at the correct height I said to him, "Now you're going into a moving part of the game that doesn't allow much time for thinking. So now you've got to think of how you are going to swing. Have you any picture of what you're going to do?"

My partner laughed. "A dozen or so," he said.

"Well, forget them, then. Just get some notion of how you are going to turn your body in swinging the club away from the ball and up over your shoulder, then remember to be slow at the top of the swing."

"Is that all?" Bill asked.

"Yes, and it may be too much. You'd probably be better off getting your club swung back any smooth way that you can and then think of only one thing specifically — hitting the ball away from you with your hands," I answered.

Bill was gripping the club fairly well and was standing up easily without being tense. He took his swing and by a lucky combination of conditions got off a drive that sent his ball approximately to where he'd aimed it in the fairway.

He looked at me with that "I've got it licked" expression you see on golfers' faces after they've hit first-class shots.

I hit my drive an easy and satisfying smack, but we will skip my shots and most of those of our opponents. The hero of this tale is Bill, and, as I told you, Bill is so much like you he should have the center of the stage at all times.

As we walked together toward his drive I considered whether I should rather cruelly deflate him and make him wake up to the fact that golf wasn't as easy as he thought it was after one accomplishment had made him jubilant.

He had ahead of him the challenging job of applying himself mentally and physically for eighty-some shots.

He would have to concentrate for about two seconds per actual shot, but before each he would have to think and decide on what was to be the object of his concentration.

This prospect would be shocking to him when he was already beginning to dream, after his good drive, that he only had to get eighteen 4s for a 72.

I didn't have the heart to tell him that no other game can beat your brains out more than golf can. Other games have only a few minutes of planned concentration and are played by instinct and reflex action most of the time.

Look at the faces of the winners of the National Open. The faces are tight, the eyes are sunk deep, and even the phenomenally resilient Hagen had the pattern of prolonged strain printed on his features. The pressure of this concentration actually turns the stomach even of a fellow who is no stranger to peril and competitive pressure.

There is almost irresistible temptation to let your mind wander in golf. But you've got to resist it and concentrate, concentrate, concentrate! Concentration in golf means that you have got to exercise the ability to make your muscles do what your mind is thinking.

In golf you've got two continuously merciless competitors: yourself and the course. If you get careless you beat yourself and the course completes your ruin. Don't expect the nature of the course to change and be more merciful to you. The course never changes in its beauty or ugliness, except when the wind is whipping — and then the change is for the worse.

But golf is still a game, emotionally, mentally and physically stimulating. It is a richly rewarding, sporting Pilgrim's Progress in which every golfer plays with Worldly Wisemen, the Shining One and Faithful, through the Enchanted Ground, past the Giant Despair and into the nineteenth hole of the Celestial City.

Bill, like every golfer, was on his way.

I haven't the faintest idea of when the famed Mulligan entered golf history, or who he was. But he certainly gave his name to one of the best shots in the game — the replay of the bad drive from the first tee. That's almost always an improved shot. If mulligans were allowed on later shots in the round some fellows would be playing all day, taking 160 strokes and counting about 80 of them.

In Scotland, when I was a lad, Mulligan never had appeared. If we missed a shot, we missed a shot and counted it, period!

When I first learned of a mulligan in American golf I was astonished. I couldn't understand the philosophy of the warm-up stroke that wasn't counted. Later I discovered the excuse for the mulligan: it was for the purpose of giving a thoughtless golfer a second chance to think.

I'd only seen my partner play one shot of the round — his comfortable drive a little over 200 yards in the middle of the fairway — but I knew from his failure to prepare thoughtfully for his drive that he would have to acquire the habit of playing his mulligans first in his brains instead of shooting, then moaning "oh, no!" and wanting another chance in which he would use his head and play the shot properly.

As we walked to where Bill was to play his second shot I saw that it called for a well-played spoon shot as the safest, surest procedure.

I asked him his intentions.

"I'm going to go for it and carry the bunker," he said, still feeling big after a moderately good drive.

Again I had to show him how his mind should take a clear look at the problem.

"The percentage is against you, and so are your eyes, I think. That trap is 180 yards away and if you do get over it you are still about 50 yards short of the green. So why don't you play the easiest possible shot? Play to the right in the short rough and you'll be set up for an easy pitch to the pin."

Bill agreed that would be the route to play without worry or risk and he stepped up to the ball.

"Are you thinking how you are going to swing?" I asked.

He assured me that he was. And he did swing well. He got his hands into the ball smartly and at the right time, but instead of going to the right the ball went to the left and into the bunker.

What went wrong? He had been stricken by the bane of all golfers. His footwork was bad and he got stuck on his right foot. When he finished his shot his right foot was flat on the ground.

He turned to me with a sad "now what?" look in his eyes.

"If the other fellows don't mind, drop another ball. Now line up your stance accurately and think of your right side and hand in hitting."

He hit the practice shot perfectly. Like many other golfers Bill had been told so much about the left side and arm and hand that he had almost forgotten the simple, obvious fact that golf is a two-handed, two-sided game. With natural coordination the dynamic action of the right-side elements and the passive functioning of the left-side elements combine into perfect, balanced technique. Maybe that explanation is too fancy. If it is, just boil it down to thinking of the left side for control and the right side for power.

As we sent the caddie to pick up the perfectly hit second shot, I remarked to Bill, "It's easy when you think."

"I thought I was thinking," he said.

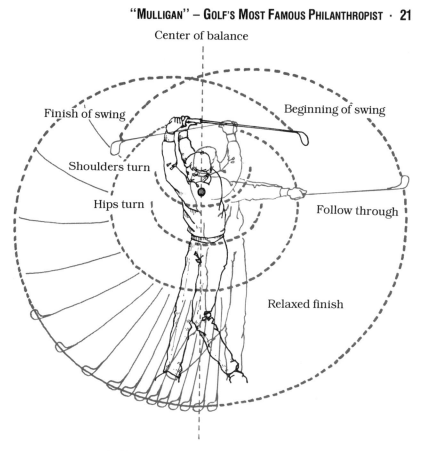

Center of balance

Finish of swing

Beginning of swing

Shoulders turn

Hips turn

Follow through

Relaxed finish

Golf is a two-handed, two-sided game

"And you were, up to the time you started to hit. Then you quit."

He argued, "I can't think about two or three things at one time."

'Then you'll probably have to experiment intelligently in locating what's the important thing to do right but that will teach you to think about your swing."

Then it struck me that Bill had played only two shots, yet had made enough mistakes to discourage anybody, so I thought I'd better cheer him.

"It takes sense and strong character for the ordinary golfer to play well. He's got a tougher job than the expert golfer who has played the shots so often that his swing is automatic. The expert can skip giving much thought to details such as the grip, the stance, footwork and getting the right side into the shot. But let me tell you from painful memory that there isn't an expert player who couldn't have won more championships by thinking of just one little thing at the right time. Everything an expert golfer does successfully is the result of thinking about what shot should be played and then concentrating on how to groove the swing properly.

"Lucky for you and other golfers that many of the points that must be thought about are details that can be taken care of correctly while you're standing still — the grip and the address, for instance. The grip is either right or wrong. There's no safe halfway point. Footwork is a different sort of problem. It is an action and you have to think of it until you get the right procedure and feeling, and keep working on it until it becomes automatic," I told Bill.

Then I hit my shot onto the green and the other fellows batted up. Bill and I walked to his ball in the bunker. I told him that if the ball was rather deep in the sand all he could do was play it as an ordinary wedge shot, keep his weight forward and get the ball out. If the ball happened to be lying clear he merely had to play it as though it were a fairway shot.

I went into those preliminaries because the sight of sand frightens many average golfers when it actually isn't any more of a hazard than some fairway and rough lies.

The lie was pretty good so I advised Bill to take an 8- or 9-iron or a wedge (whichever club he could play most confidently), set his feet firmly in the sand with his weight a bit heavier on his left foot and, without turning his body, hit the ball on the downstroke.

I impressed on him that he was to stand almost still but not stiff, swing the arms back a little, bend the wrists only slightly, and hit into the sand. By all means he must remember to hit the ball before the club went into the sand.

Bill was very attentive. He gripped the club firmly without being tense and he played a nice little punch shot that landed fifteen or twenty feet from the pin.

He looked apologetically at me and said, "I should have been nearer." I made no reply. I've seen times when I could have used a shot as good as that one.

The other fellows appeared to be surprised that Bill was not contented with his shot, but they said nothing. It was beginning to strike me that I was teaching a class instead of limiting myself to Bill, showing him how to play better golf and enjoy it keenly by applying a bit more of his IQ to the game.

So I thought I'd better let Bill satisfy himself that my thinking was sound about the way to play the shot from that trap to the green.

"Why don't you play the shot again?" I suggested.

"Can I play it my way?" Bill asked.

"Certainly."

I quietly remarked to Ed, who had halted on his way to the second tee, "I know how he will play it. He will stay back on his right leg, try to pick the ball clean and flip it onto the green. But I don't know how the shot will come out."

Bill rolled another ball into the bunker, played the shot just as I had forecast to Ed, and the ball went to within a few inches of the cup. Bill strutted out of the trap. He felt that he had improved on my technique.

I had to laugh; Bill was so highly self-satisfied.

"Play it again," I said.

"Why?"

"Because you now are trying to show me how to play. Before I get insulted I want to see you replay that shot your way."

He rolled another ball into the trap and it was lying nicely on top of the sand. He stepped up to the ball, swung and dubbed the shot entirely. He left the ball in the sand.

The short punch shot from a good lie in a trap

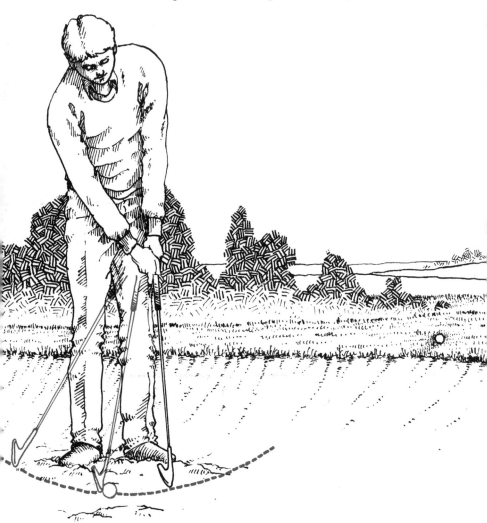

Ball played off right heel, feet planted firmly, no body turn, weight slightly on left foot; Club meets ball first — sand afterward

"That's your way, and all you could expect. The proper shot was the one that you played first when you were a little in front of the ball, when the ball was about in line with your right heel and when your left arm and the shaft of your club were in line at address. Your second shot — that one you almost holed — was an accident. After that you reverted to the brainless system and just hoped on the shot. The ball didn't come up."

Then we walked up to Bill's first ball out of the trap and I looked over the line of the putt that was a little less than twenty feet. "What do you figure on this one?" I inquired.

"Oh, it's a little uphill and it will fall away left to right on a slope."

My observation confirmed Bill's.

I said to him, "Now let's see you miss it on the left side, the top side of the hole. Stroke that putt smoothly but don't move your head the breadth of one hair. If you miss then, O.K., but if you move your head you haven't got a chance to hole the putt or any excuse if you do miss it."

I didn't tell him anything about holding the putter. Any grip that is comfortable, that makes use of the tactile sense in the finger tips for control and that gets the face of the putter squarely across the line of the putt as the ball is stroked is a good grip.

Keeping the head steady and the face of the putter at a right angle to the line of the putt are the two essentials of putting. Everything else is individual style. The speed of the green and the touch or force of the putt are factors that can't be taught or even helpfully described, except to the extent that the length of the backswing of a putter may determine the length that the putt will travel.

Bill wasn't able to force himself to keep thinking. His putt went three feet beyond the hole and passed on the low side.

When a player misses sidehill putts on the low side he never is even close to making the putt, but if he misses on the high side every time that he does miss, he is bound to be a beautiful putter. The odds of holing plenty of those high-side putts favor him.

I recalled that Joe Kirkwood, who was one of the finest and most underrated players, was putting badly in the British Open at Troon in 1923. Arthur Havers won that with 295, Hagen was second at 296, Mac Smith was third at 297, and Kirkwood finished fourth with 298, taking 69 for his third round and 78 for his final eighteen. During the last round Joe asked me why he was missing so many putts that he normally would make. I told him he was missing them all on the bottom side. If he'd rolled those putts on the high side of the hole he would have won that championship.

Kirkwood was usually a smart golfer. Recalling his tragedy at Troon I couldn't blame Bill too much for making the lowside mistake here.

Bill holed his three-footer, coming back for a 5. That was par for his grade of golf. Jim and Ed got 5s, with only one mechanical error and three mental lapses figuring in their total of ten strokes, but I wasn't coaching them and didn't have to push their heads into the game.

I talked myself into being Exhibit A for Bill to imitate, didn't make any mistakes, and had the good luck to get a birdie with a twelve-foot putt that climbed uphill and ran into the cup as though it had eyes and brains.

For his mental efforts on the first hole I could give Bill only about 50 per cent. He didn't think about his drive. He did think while he was hitting his third shot. He was about 50-50 on his first putt. He was too high to have a chance to hole the putt, but he didn't go so far past and on such an incline that he would have a delicate and dangerous putt coming back.

While the four of us and our caddies were walking toward the second tee I asked Bill if he wanted to call off the deal for using his muscle and my mind to take the opposition's money.

He was emphatic. "I'm all for keeping at it." He added that he believed he'd used his head more in playing one hole of golf than he had in playing during the previous two months.

"Do you fellows want to keep on with us?" I asked Ed and Jim.

"O. K. with me," Jim declared. "Some of it might rub off on me.

"Nobody is on the tee yet. We're not holding anybody back. And what have I got to lose except money? Help Bill all you can, but don't embarrass me by asking me to use my brains," said Ed.

Barring the loss of time for Bill's extra shots out of the trap, the processes of counseling and thinking about the shots had added less than five minutes to the time Bill might ordinarily take in playing the hole. In that brief extra period he'd begun to get an exciting glimpse of what a different and delightful game golf could be for him.

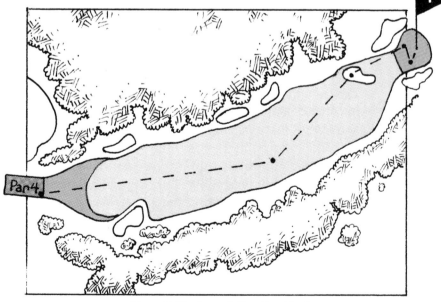

How Bill played the first hole

*T*he second hole is the same type of hole as our first, except that the bend of the dogleg is from left to right, and the hole is about sixty yards shorter than the first.

We're going to skip the details of how our opposition played these holes. I've got enough to do in reporting on my partner.

I said to Bill, "Now here you are expected to show progress. What percentage of your mentality did you use in playing the first hole?"

Bill didn't answer directly. He mumbled, "I did the best I knew how," and held out a hand to his caddie for the ball the boy had taken out of the washer.

"No hurry. Tell me what you learned playing the first hole," I asked.

"I learned where to tee the ball. I learned that I should pay more attention to my footwork in aiming and playing the shot. I got an idea about how to play a bunker shot and, if I miss a putt, to miss it on the high side of the hole."

I nodded.

"Have I got to think that hard every hole, and every round?" Bill sighed.

"No, but you'll have to use your head a whole lot more than you have been doing. You have to do that until you train yourself. Then a good deal of the brain work will be done subconsciously. You won't be another Jones but you will be able to get around a course."

That prospect seemed to cheer him. Anyway, he laughed. I could almost see what was going on in his mind. He thought I was going to continue thinking his shots for him until I had

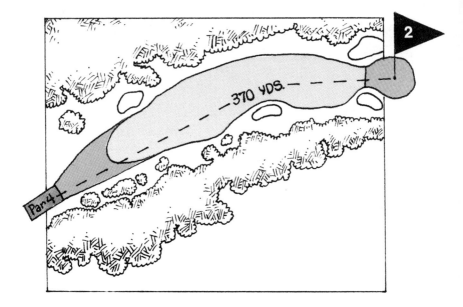

him hypnotized and by some magic he would keep on playing with my head. I blasted that pretty dream, quickly and cruelly.

"On the first hole I helped you. Now, in playing this hole, you are on your own. You should have a notion of what it's all about."

He wasn't bothered. He promptly proved that it had been a wasted effort to tell him where he should tee, considering the strategy of the hole. He walked to the right side of the second tee, bent over and pegged his ball up for his drive.

I didn't comment on this case of flunking a lesson. He should have played the ball from the left side of the tee to make the fairway as wide as he could get it.

He stood up to the ball well. His grip was careful and fairly good. He took a nice swing, smooth and in good balance and with some rhythm and zing to it.

The ball took off in a fine flight with a little bit of a hook that would have been most acceptable if he had used his head in selecting a place to tee his drive.

His drive landed in the rough to the left of the fairway. In incorrectly teeing the ball he had cut down the angle that should be figured in giving oneself an ample margin of error.

"A fine tee shot," I remarked. "The rough isn't bad."

"Yeah, but what bad luck to have a drive like that get into the rough. That must have cost me ten to twenty yards," my partner wailed.

"Not bad luck, bad judgment," I remarked. "I told you about teeing your drive so you'd give your shot plenty of space in the clear."

Bill softly and earnestly declared himself to be a stupid so-and-so.

"This is no time for character analysis," I reminded him. "You are not in bad shape. The ball is lying well."

He was 160 or 170 yards from the green. Guarding the green were bunkers to the right and left. The left-side trap was the deeper one and it was farther from the green than the trap on the right side.

The target for the shot was narrow. Unless Bill hit a shot that he could make about once in five tries he didn't have a chance of knocking the ball between the bunkers and onto the green.

He lost his concentration — his capacity to regard the situation thoughtfully and make the right decision. Deceived into a hasty move by an easy-looking lie he took out a 3-wood and stepped up to the ball.

Then he did what he'd probably been doing often during the rounds that had disgusted him with his golf.

Instead of making a swing he heaved himself at the ball.

"Heave" is one of the ugliest words in golf. Maybe you think "shank" or its synonym "socket" is the most revolting word. "Heave" is worse. It is what the average golfer does so often that he makes the game much more work than the Scots intended it to be.

I am an American who really knows the Scots, having been

born one of them. The Scotch accent on thrift applies more to abhorrence of unnecessary effort than to pain at loose spending of money. This certainly isn't because a Scot has any laziness in his blood; it is because making a living in the lean and holy land of Scotia and fishing off its shores is hard enough

The body has been "lifted" and thrown forward

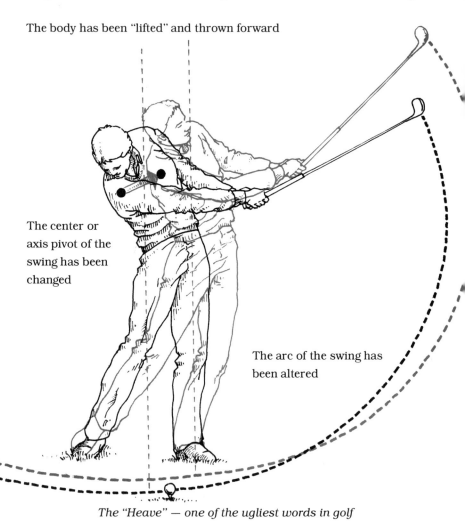

The center or axis pivot of the swing has been changed

The arc of the swing has been altered

The "Heave" — one of the ugliest words in golf

labor at its easiest. It is nothing to encourage making work of a game.

A definition of "heave" in the dictionary to which I have turned is "lift and throw." That's exactly what Bill did. He lifted himself until he slanted like the leaning tower of Pisa at the top of his backswing. There he tottered, hopelessly out of balance, after which he threw himself at the ball in a frantic, futile manner.

The club, held so tightly that all Bill could do with it was make a stiff-armed poke, dug into the grass under the ball and the shot turned out to be a high pop fly to the left and farther into the rough.

Like so many unthinking golfers, Bill had made the primary mistake of using the wrong club for the shot. He should have taken a 4- or 5-wood and settled wisely for smacking the ball up and out of the rough with an easy shot short of the green and to a safe spot from which he would have had a decent chance to get close enough to the hole for one putt and his par 4.

But here was our hero, lying 2, in thick deep grass and with approximately 120 yards to go to the hole. The best he possibly could do from there was to play a perfect shot and take two putts for a 5. He might play a dumb shot and struggle for a 7.

I guessed what he might do and I watched in pained suspense as he proceeded to substantiate my fears.

He took out a 5-iron. With that club and from that lie Hagen and Hogan together couldn't have played a good recovery shot.

Bill was panicky. He tightened up from his head to his toes, heaved himself at the ball again and bumped it about twenty yards ahead.

He had the glassy look of a man lying on the canvas and having 9 counted over him.

Bill began sending up distress signals. "I am sinking fast. What should I play?"

"Sorry, friend, but this is a hole you are playing on your own. Use just a little bit of brains and figure out your own way of getting to shore."

It took a little self-discipline and mental energy to get the right answer and Bill came up with them. The ball wasn't lying badly. It was one of those shots that entice a fellow to try to hit them harder than they need to be hit instead of hitting them squarely. Bill didn't fall for the lure. He picked out an approach wedge, stayed in front of the ball, took an upright swing and knocked down at the ball. He did exactly what was required to make the shot and when he eventually looked up the ball was only about five yards or so off the green.

He'd got more distance than he usually could expect to get from a wedge. By playing the ball about even with his right toe and having his hands well ahead of the shot he closed the face of the club so it connected with less than normal wedge loft.

Right here I want to tell you something that I hope will remind you to use your own knowledge and judgment in picking a club for a certain shot rather than being governed by what some other fellow does.

I've been with several fellows watching golf tournaments on television when the announcer whispers that the player on the screen is using a 4-iron for a 190-yard shot, a wedge for a 150-yard shot, or some other club for a distance considerably beyond what the fair or even the rather good golfer could get using the club under normal conditions.

My companions will gasp and express blazing desires to get similar distances from their clubs. Later, as I have observed, they will fall all over themselves trying to outclub the experts.

What my friends haven't noticed is the type of shot being played and whether the clubface is manipulated into less than its normal loft as the ball is hit. They don't know the wind and turf and topographical conditions that have influenced the

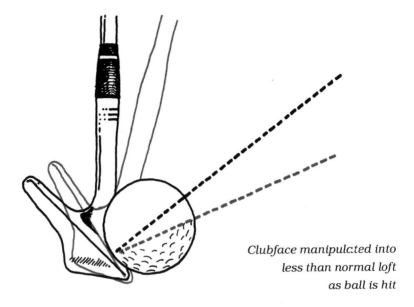

Clubface manipulated into
less than normal loft
as ball is hit

choice of the club and the way of playing the shot. They further don't know that often playing stars alter the lofts of their irons so the irons, by numbers, are not of orthodox specifications.

Do your own thinking about what club to use. You may delight yourself and profoundly impress the onlookers and opposition.

I can recollect a pleasant and possibly historic case to illustrate my point.

I was paired with a personable and competent lad in a tournament at Oklahoma City in the late twenties. We got to a short hole where it was my honor. Quite audibly, but apparently casually, I asked my caddie for a club that was more than adequate for the shot. By cutting and otherwise finessing the shot I got the ball into the center of the green. I thought that if my fellow competitor hit a good shot with the same club he'd be over the green, over the road and, maybe, over Oklahoma into Texas.

But the other fellow did just what I'm advising you to do. All by himself he decided on the club to use. He paid no attention to my Machiavellian suggestion. He took a club two or three numbers less than the one I'd used as bait and knocked the ball right into the hole for an ace. That gave him the margin that he held to the finish in winning his first major money tournament.

The youth was my friend Horton Smith. Countless times after the amusing and convincing demonstration Horton put on at Oklahoma City I saw other examples of his headwork.

He played his own game when I put him to the test. I play my own game. You play yours in using the correct club for the job that is to be done.

But let's get back to Bill. We left him about five yards short of the second green.

The recollection of the two shots he had wasted by sheer stupidity haunted him. He couldn't stop thinking about what had happened and begin thinking only about what to do with the next shot.

The ball was lying nicely on the fairway. The hole was on the back of a green that sloped uphill. Bill asked me what club to play.

"This is still your hole. I want to see if you can think," I replied.

Thus deserted, Bill picked out the wedge again, flipped it with his wrists instead of swinging it back a bit, and scooped the ball fifteen feet short of the pin. The job was an exhibition of a crippling lack of thought.

In the first place, taking a wedge to lift a shot that would fall into the sloping face of the green showed that not the slightest attention had been paid to the trajectory of the shot. It was bound to come to a quick stop. A 5-, 6- or 7-iron chip, played practically like a putt, would run uphill and be much more reliable than the wedge in keeping the ball pretty close to the line of the hole.

When the wedge pitch plunked into the green far short of

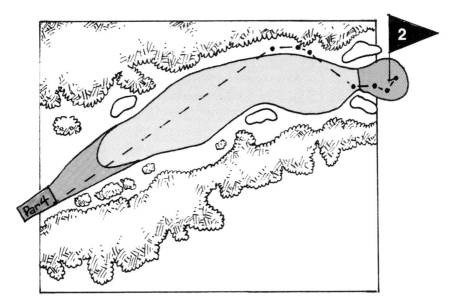

How Bill played the second hole

where Bill vaguely hoped it would get, he groaned, "I've had enough."

"Oh, no; you don't quit with my money riding on you," I told him. "Get up there and putt."

His mind was in a turmoil by now. His head moved on the putt and he missed by a wide margin, on the wrong side of the hole and considerably past it, so he had a downhill, sidehill putt coming back. He tapped that nervously and gently and, of course, missed. He had taken an 8 on the hole.

Bill appealed to me. "Have we got to play the whole round?"

We all answered him with laughs and no pity at all.

"You are a multimillionaire, so I've heard. I don't know how you made it and I'm amazed that you've got any of it." While we walked to the third tee I began giving Bill the between-the-halves talk of the hard coach. "If business sense were like golf sense you would be caddying here instead of belonging to a fine club and playing today."

"You're rough on me," Bill protested. "I'm trying my best to learn."

"I'm rough on you? What do you think this is doing to me? What if this turns out to be a waste of my time, money and reputation? If you resist my pleas, threats and tutoring to get you to think, you can keep on playing a brainless game but you'll wreck me." Bill was beginning to grin. "Hook yourself together or I will be just an old broken-down pro dreaming of the proud and happy days before I met you."

"Come on, fellows," Ed pleaded, "Tommy's putt saved you the honors. Bat up. Armour is getting in a dramatic mood. He may begin, 'It is an ancient golfer and he stoppeth one of three.' Then we never will get back to the locker room."

As I reached into my bag for a club I said to Ed, "I'm here only in the interests of good clean fun and your money, so we'll move along. For your money my partner will play the third hole with his muscle and this ancient golfer's brain."

My partner seemed relieved. He didn't know that I was trying to think what I could say or do to make him develop and use some golf brains.

In a friendly round such as the four of us were playing I didn't have to think much about my own game. I'd been at golf long enough so my reflexes automatically handled most situations correctly, but thinking about another fellow's game was proving harder work for me than it was for Bill.

It's not the walking or the swinging that tires you at golf; it's the thinking or, more often, the ineffectual effort of trying to think and not knowing how to do it that wears you down.

I didn't want to complicate matters for Bill by giving him a refresher course on the fundamentals of golfing technique as we were going along, but his grip could stand improvement.

The grips of the other two fellows weren't ideal, either, although Ed had quite a good connection with the club, barring a tendency to weaken a little with his left hand on his power shots. When that happens there's usually a hook, and some self-nominated diagnostician will say, "He overpowered it with his right hand." The diagnosis is 180 degrees incorrect. What happened is that the shot was underpowered by the left hand. I don't know of a golfer who can put too much right hand into a shot if his left hand is correspondingly applied to the shot.

This is as good a place as any to halt our playing lesson to Bill and consider the all-important subject of the grip.

There are very few golfers who don't need to check up on their grips now and then.

Most of the experts frequently appraise their grips and come up with valuable discoveries and corrections. A couple of years ago I had pointed out to me by Claude Harmon a flaw that had developed in my grip. After so many years of holding a club about as well as a mortal could be expected to, I'd got careless, I suppose, and my hands were not staying together at the top of the swing. I was momentarily losing control of the club. The instant that was brought to my attention I corrected the fault.

In 1957 Jimmy Demaret had a great year for a veteran, being high up among tournament circuit money winners and being only one stroke behind Dick Mayer and Cary Middlecoff in the National Open that Mayer won in a playoff. Jimmy said that the only deliberate change in his game that he could think of as accounting for his improved performance was gripping the club just a tiny bit more to the right than he previously had held his hands on the grip.

The three amateurs with whom I was playing hardly did the first thing about the grip that a good player does invariably, and that is to get the club cradled snugly on the roots of his fingers. When the club is at that point where the fingers and the palm meet, the fingers can curl around the grip so the sensitive fingertips can communicate the feeling of a good swing to the rest of the player's nervous system.

Some day, I suppose, some intense student of golf will write a thesis on this subject of fingertip control of the golf swing. Maybe you are old enough to remember the story, play and song of Jimmy Valentine, the safecracker, who found the combination with his fingertips. The successful golfer, like Jimmy Valentine, finds the answer with his fingertips.

There was too much pressure and tension in Bill's grip when he was addressing his shots. The grip should be light but firm, at address. If the grip is squeezed when you address the ball, by the time you get to the top of the swing your grip will be lifeless and you won't be able to swing the club with zip coming down into the ball. Another thing: When you are holding the club with practically a *rigor mortis* grip at the top of the backswing you will loosen at the ball and hit a flabby blow.

You've got to learn just how gently you can hold the club without losing control of it at the top of the backswing. When you have an easy but secure hold of the club as you begin your downswing you will spontaneously strengthen the grip as you hit into the ball.

In my book *How to Play Your Best Golf All the Time*, you get all the basic information you need about the *V*s of your thumbs and forefingers pointing to the right shoulder as the grip for the average-to-fairly-good golfer.

The fellows with whom I was playing might have made good use of the reminder that turning the hands slightly to the right on the circumference of the grip tends to produce a hook. When the hands of the average golfer are a bit to the left on the shaft so the Vs are vertical or slightly to the left the shot probably will be a slice. There are other causes of a slice but the hands being even slightly on the left of the shaft as you look down at them at address is the slicing grip. I don't think that anybody wants to slice except as an emergency measure in trouble. However, when you know why you may be slicing (or hooking) you can correct your grip if misplaced grip is the cause of the curving shot.

You also will get a slice if you hit the ball with your club coming from outside the line of flight and slicing across the ball, due to body or arm action, or from an open stance; but in most cases the average golfer's slice is caused primarily by his grip.

The grip is exceedingly important because it is with your hands that you whip the ball away from you. That's the only possible way of getting a shot that amounts to anything.

Bill was inclined to have a grip weakness that is common among golfers. His right thumb and forefinger didn't stay as close together as they should. Hence, at the top of his backswing his club would slip down in the V of his right hand.

He didn't realize that the right forefinger and thumb are a key combination in the grip. They account for giving the clubhead a great deal of the lash that comes in the critical sector at the bottom of the swing when the hands are almost up to the ball and the wrists have just begun to uncock.

The right forefinger curls around the shaft in a sort of trigger grip. The inner part of the ball of the right thumb is securely pressing on the grip material but not pressing so heavily that the tip of the thumbnail touches. Not one detail of the grip ever should be so tight that you feel tension in your forearms.

Without being aware of it my partner was fighting a tendency that is the curse of the literate golfer. Many of these fellows who have read quite a little about golf become so intent on left hand, left arm and left side functioning that the right-side elements are almost neglected. They go at the job of shotmaking negatively and drag the clubhead into the ball.

In their hurry to get playing about nine out of ten golfers neglect to learn that the left hand guides the club (with the left arm being the radius of the swing) and the right hand does the hitting.

You've got to guide the club into the groove and you can't do a good job of guiding and hitting with the same hand.

You can hold the club a little bit firmer with the fingers of the left hand than with those of the right to get control. The last two fingers of the left hand are especially snug on the club. The right-hand grip will instinctively strengthen as the ball is hit.

Nobody except a southpaw can hit a golf shot very far with just the left hand. I've been in debates on that subject and have seen that shots of 100 yards made with only the left hand holding the driver will usually win all the wagers.

The grip and the stance can be taken care of while you are standing still. When you know what you are doing and are careful you shouldn't have trouble with them.

But the control of the path of the club is a difficult job. To do that you've got to have your hands and feet neatly coordinated and you've got to remember to hit the ball when the time comes.

If your grip of the club is strong but flexible your wrists will be limber. They will be cocked correctly by the centrifugal force of the clubhead and they'll automatically straighten out at the bottom of the swing. When your grip restricts natural wrist action your shot will become only a stiff arm and body push.

The sound of the clubhead meeting the ball usually is an accurate indicator of the character of the grip. If the club hits the ball with a crack that sounds like a rifle shot you may be confident that you have a firm, flexible finger grip. If the sound of the club hitting the ball is a dull and feeble plop then you'd better work on correcting your grip.

I've had interesting experiences with sports headliners who have exhibited the general inclination to clutch the golf club much too tightly. The case of Stan Musial comes to mind.

Musial holds a baseball bat loosely, waggling it so freely you'd almost think he had rubber fingers and wrists. As the pitch is delivered Musial never tightly clutches the bat but swings it smoothly until the precisely timed instant when his grip subconsciously adjusts to required firmness and his hands lash the bat against the ball.

At golf "The Man" is prone to go at the small, still ball with a notion to overpower it. He will grip the club so hard at the top of the backswing he almost presses the shaft flat. He gets so tight he sticks at the top of the swing.

All I have to say to him to get him to lighten his grip and allow his hands to work and put life into his swing is, "How much do you think you'd hit if you held a bat as tightly as you're holding that golf club?"

While playing golf with Otto Graham I've asked him if he gripped a football tightly when he swung his arm back to pass. He answered that he was barely holding onto the ball.

In golf, as in most other games I can think of — baseball, football, tennis, bowling, billiards, croquet and horseshoe pitching — tightness of grip often ruins the chance of first-class performance. When the actual moment of hitting or throwing comes, the light grip will firm up automatically, and you'll get your power.

I couldn't make any major alterations in Bill's grip or swing with the third hole facing us. His errors and those of our opponents did suggest that I discuss the grip at this point in

Right thumb and forefinger close
— grip without tension

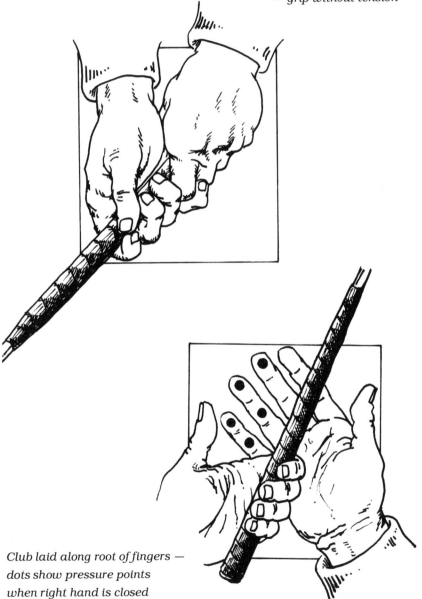

Club laid along root of fingers —
dots show pressure points
when right hand is closed

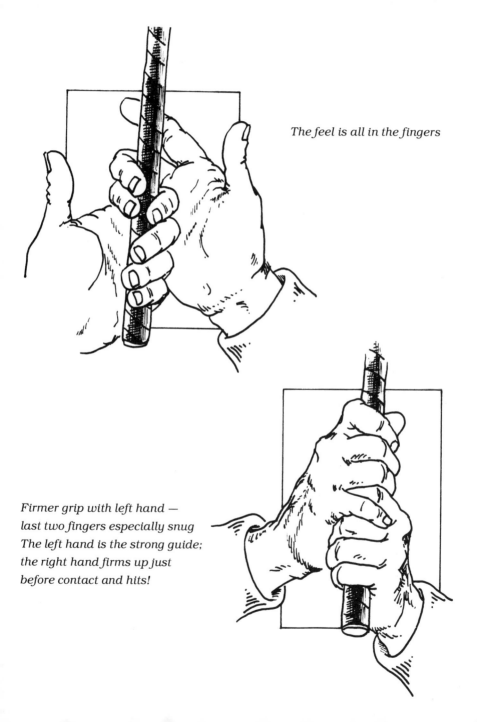

The feel is all in the fingers

*Firmer grip with left hand —
last two fingers especially snug
The left hand is the strong guide;
the right hand firms up just
before contact and hits!*

my book, so you might be moved to examine how you connect yourself with your club. You may find that your grip is the cause of about half your golfing trouble.

*T*he third hole of our course is around 200 yards. It's a straightaway hole, showing practically no imagination in its design but a lot of shovel in its construction around the green.

There are deep and steep bunkers right and left of an alley of ten yards or so that feed into the green.

About all you've got to do in playing this hole mentally is to use the right club off the tee.

I put the problem up to Bill this way:

"Suppose you were playing this hole for a thousand dollars, what club would you use?"

Bill deliberated, then said he'd use a driver.

"With a driver you haven't got enough margin for error. Five yards off the line on either side and you are in a bunker. You lack the ability and reliability to get yourself out of the sand with only one shot, especially if you'd have to get the ball up quickly from traps like those ahead. If it's O. K. with the other fellows, you play the tee shot my way with a 4-wood — then play another one your way with a driver."

The way I figured it for my partner was that with a 4-wood he probably would be short and safe and would have an easy pitch or chip to get him close enough for one putt. Then he'd get the par 3 that an average golfer must make on the majority of the short holes if he is to have a decent score.

Bill took a 4-wood and swung it smoothly. He didn't have to be nervous, hurried and tight. If his shot went wrong it was my fault. I had picked the club for him and he could blame me.

Logically, then, the percentage was with the 4-wood. The

ball smacked nicely from the club and went about 180 yards right down the middle.

"Now, your way." I got his driver from his caddie and handed it to Bill.

He went at the assignment cautiously. Everything was going well until he got a little too eager. Before he'd actually finished his backswing he fell forward, then pushed the ball into the right bunker.

In a high-nosed, satisfied way, I looked at Bill.

"Do you agree?"

Bill nodded. "You must know something."

"I know what we are trying to do and you don't."

I've got to say for Bill, though, that there are very few average golfers who have such good judgment and restraint they voluntarily will play short on a par-3 hole and outsmart the hole instead of trying to outmuscle it.

We walked up to the ball Bill had played with the 4-wood. He had an uphill approach to the hole similar to that he'd had at the preceding hole and that he had misplayed by using a wedge.

Bill looked at me for instruction. He got it.

"Now take your 6-iron. Play the ball off your right foot. Address it with your weight on your left foot and keep it there all through your swing. You don't need much of a swing. Just swing your arms back until your hands are about in line with your right hip. Let your wrists cock a little. They'll do that automatically. Then swing your arms down with your shoulders. Your wrists will spontaneously uncock about the time your hands are directly in front of you. That will be the delayed hand action you hear talked about."

He made a feeble attempt at controversy, thinking that he might do better with a more lofted club. The ordinary golfer loves to argue.

"We're all lucky," I said to Bill. "We've hit a lull in play this afternoon. Nobody's pushing us and you are making money while I'm giving you lessons for which others of the upper classes have paid thousands of dollars. Our playmates really are paying for this. They aren't kicking. They're learning something, too. So I tell you what to do and you want to teach me. That's what happens to pros. I am glad I can afford to argue with you for amusement."

"O.K. What now?" Bill stepped up to the ball with his 6-iron.

"Keep your left arm straight and hit that ball nice and firmly."

He chipped it up smartly, about eight feet from the cup.

"Now let's see you play that drive of yours from the bunker."

Bill walked down into the cavernous trap where his drive had rolled a couple of feet from the green side of the trap.

"You've got to bring this one out with a steep rise. The ball has got to get up quickly. Now let's see your way of doing that. You know what the problem is; go to it."

He stood behind the ball, playing it ahead of his left foot. His weight was on his right leg. His stance was closed so, naturally, he took the club back far inside the line of flight that he should have visualized. He threw himself at the ball. His wedge buried into the sand. The ball was bumped out and against the bank of the bunker from which it rebounded and dribbled almost into its original lie.

That's a humiliating sort of shot. It's a bunker shot that the ordinary golfer plays far too often.

"Let's try it now the easy way, which is the only way to get a shot like that up and nicely onto the green every time. Play the ball off your left heel and keep your weight pretty well on your left foot. Open your stance a little and grip so you open the blade of your wedge. You should be facing to the right of the hole. Got all that?"

Bill nodded.

"Now comes the gimmick. Play this shot with absolutely no body or head movement. Keep the left arm straight. Swing from your left shoulder and splash the ball out of the sand with your hands. You've got to have the club coming from outside the line in toward you. And by all that you hold holy, follow through!"

Bill made a hurried, frightened hack at the ball, lost his balance, and again batted the ball against the bank of the bunker.

"That's partially my fault," I consoled Bill. "I should have spelled it out for you. I should have told you to hit behind the ball and never quit on the shot. Your wedge has got to go through the sand and under the ball so a cushion of sand will throw the ball right out of the bunker. When the average golfer is in a deep bunker he should plan and play to get the ball onto the green and not try any fancy business or daydreaming about getting the ball into the hole."

"This is positively the easiest shot in golf," I continued. "Now set yourself as you know you should, draw a bead on a spot a couple of inches behind the ball, fire away and finish the shot."

And to prove it is an easy shot (also to show that Bill and I both are lucky at times), Bill whacked his third try inches from the hole.

"That ends that lesson. Remember it. Now let's see if the money ball that we're playing my way can be masterminded into the cup. Look this putt over carefully and tell me what you see."

"It's a left-to-right putt and the borrow calls for me aiming it about an inch to the left of the hole, on the high side," Bill decided.

"Let's aim it about three inches to the left. Are you sure that you've got the face of the putter squared to the line of the putt, or is it squarely across a line directly to the hole?"

Bill checked his aim and discovered, as most golfers usually do, that he had placed his putter with its face square to the hole. After rectifying this sighting error he stroked the ball smoothly and as I was watching his head stay still I knew that the putt was exactly on its way home.

He got his 3 the easy, sensible way, with a foolproof tee shot, an approach that didn't require any pronounced skill or delicacy, and a putt that was holed by taking advantage of gravity.

There was mild and strictly formal beefing by the opposition when we counted Bill's 3 with the ball that Bill and I played as an entry. Taking advantage of the rare absence of pressing traffic on the course, Ed had

How Bill played the third hole

gone into the right-hand trap and played a couple of practice shots out following the directions I'd given Bill.

The shots popped out so well that Ed remarked he was reconciled to being robbed of cash as long as he learned something that might help him to steal from others.

On that high moral note we proceeded toward the fourth tee.

*A*fter playing one hole with his thinking and execution and two holes with my thinking and his shotmaking, Bill was beginning to get the big idea. The big idea is that golf can be made easier and better by using the head of the golfer as well as the head of the club.

He looked like a golfer as he stood up to his drive on the fourth tee. He thought like one, too.

Our fourth hole is 410 yards. It's a somewhat dull hole, simply straight ahead. This day the wind was at our backs.

On a hole like our fourth with a wide fairway you can set your ball up any place on the tee. You don't have to concern yourself with playing cautiously.

To my astonishment and delight Bill took out a 2-wood, the correct club for a drive with a favoring wind. He teed the ball up medium high in the center of the tee.

He acted relaxed. His knees and shoulders looked limber without being floppy and weak.

When you are playing with the wind you have a feeling that if you'll just hit the ball easily — but hit it — the wind will supply the power.

Bill made a real good-looking turn. His footwork and knee action were smooth and rotated his body around a stable axis. The inner part of his left shoulder slid nicely under his chin. He made his swing in velvety tempo.

The ball took off with a sharp smack and in a graceful, long trajectory. The shot had a lot of class to it. Bill, like most golfers in the 15-22 handicap range, could hit at least four out of five of his drives as competently as he'd hit this shot off

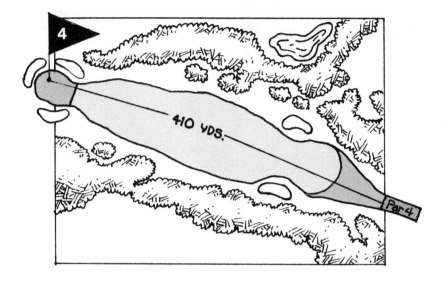

the fourth tee. But fellows of this type lose big shots because they neglect to get organized and unlocked so they can pivot freely, swing the arms and throw the clubhead into the ball with their hands. Too often they fail to stay loose enough to allow the normal hitting action to get started, take place and be completed — all without any restriction.

Well, here was Bill's model drive, 210 to 220 yards right on the beam. If he had been allowed to carry the ball and place it down the fairway as his drive he wouldn't have had nerve enough to spot the ball any better, except for one detail. The lie was close. It was not so close that it should present any difficulty to a player who was accustomed to playing the ball as it lies, but it was close enough to be a problem to the fellow who always wants to play "winter rules" and improve his lies.

Before I get away from this topic of improving the lie of the ball I want to say that I don't know of any one thing that has made it tougher for the average golfer to master the making of well-executed shots than the national custom of playing "winter rules" with the faintest excuse or, actually, none at all. Learn to hit the shots that present some reason for concentrating on a problem, and you'll get into the habit of playing all shots better.

Now, back to Bill as he looked over the close-lying ball that was about 190 yards away from the green.

Such a shot would involve no trouble at all for the expert. He would merely have smashed down so the clubface would get under the ball. With the helping wind the shot would have gone off like a missile.

The tendency of the ordinary golfer is to try to hit too hard when he's got a shot of 180 to 200 yards to make. That's what makes the holes of about 400 yards punishing to the majority of golfers.

I would have taken a 3-wood from that lie.

Bill took out a 4-wood. I was getting a dawning pride in the fellow. He was playing it safe, simple and smart. With the following wind there wouldn't be much difference between a 3-wood and a 4-wood shot.

I looked quizzically at my friend, wondering if he was developing a golf brain or if he was just lucky.

He told me, "I'm going to play this as though it were an iron shot. I'll play it halfway between my feet and make my swing more upright so I'll hit down at the ball."

Bill did all right. He was careful about getting the ball in correct relation to his feet (which is something that most golfers don't do) and he kept his weight a bit heavier on his left foot so he would be disposed to incline the plane of his swing slightly more upright than it would be for a shot from a good lie.

He didn't get the ball flying high through the air, but he did hit it solidly with the face of his club a bit closed. The ball shot out as a low liner and finished on the green. Bill was more than contented and ready to take bows. He asked, "Was that it, Tommy?"

"Fine. And much less effort than playing it stupid. All you had to do was to think a bit, hit the ball first and then let the

*The stance for the 4-wood
shot from a close lie*

projecting bottom part of that 4-wood go along skimming the turf and finish while you stayed solidly balanced. You smacked that one correctly with your hands."

The ball came to rest thirty feet from the hole. The putt was a tricky, curling, right-to-left roll with a little hill in front of the hole.

He did pretty well with his first putt. He didn't survey it fore and aft and sideways and bend, kneel and sprawl on the green until he got himself so confused and jittery that he couldn't get a picture of the putt into his mind.

He did what any intelligent man who knows the first thing about physiology and psychology would do. He lined up the putt in a general way and kept himself thinking of about how far the putt had to go. By thinking specifically only of the distance and lining up the putter face and his stance in a general sort of way, Bill was able to keep himself relaxed.

His first putt finished two feet to the left of the hole. There followed a tediously careful job of surveying the remaining two feet. Bill allowed himself plenty of time for working up extreme tension on this putt. I was surprised that he was able to tap it instead of hitting it with a nervous jerk to the side of the hole and past it.

"This looks to me like a delicate left-to-right putt," he remarked after his reconnaissance. Then he proceeded to putt and the ball stayed to the left as it passed the hole.

I felt a stab in my own bosom when Bill missed that putt and his chance for a par. The third putt he holed. It was as risky as the one he'd just blown but he played it right into the hole without any dainty and fancy business or finesse.

"Isn't that pitiful?" he groaned. "I hit a fine drive. Even you admitted that I used my brains in making a second shot much better than I usually can hit a 4-wood. The first putt got me almost close enough for a 'gimme.' I was very careful with it and I blew it!"

"I'm honestly sorry for you. Just one short moment and

your head that had been wide awake all the rest of the route went to sleep."

"And where did I stop thinking? I played every shot with brains," my partner insisted.

"Except that two-foot putt. There is very, very rarely any borrow on a two-foot putt. I'll take a chance at saying there's no such a thing as borrow on a putt that short. You must putt it right straight into the hole. You have got to show confidence in keeping the putt on the line instead of trying to get too cute. If you do try to nurse the putt you will touch the ball so gently that it can't possibly stay on the line."

Bill looked mournfully at the ball. "You dirty little ---------," he muttered. "But I've got to say for you that gentlemen generally give me putts longer than the one I just missed."

"Gentlemen golfers don't," I replied. Silently we walked off the green.

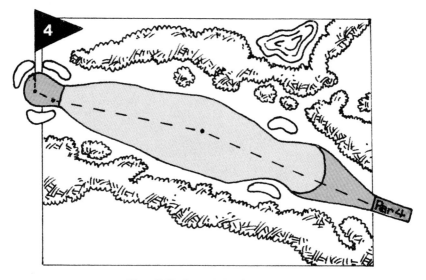

How Bill played the fourth hole

*T*he par-5 holes break the heads, hearts and backs of typical golfers. The heads are not broken by being overstrained.

Our 540-yard fifth hole is an exhibit of the sort of par 5 that the average golfer tries to murder by brute force and by which he gets murdered with a 7 or 8.

The hole begins by giving you a good chance. The correct drive should be a right-to-left shot. That allows the player room for the hook that may result when the player tries too strenuously for distance and by luck alone doesn't smother the shot.

Bill teed his ball on the right side. That was a wise start. It was my turn to direct the playing of this hole, so after the ball was teed I asked Bill about the plan of his campaign.

He replied that he was going to try to keep on the right side of the fairway, stay back of the ball while he was swinging, and hit it away with his hands.

He went through the motions in unhurried tempo and cracked his drive about 210 yards and to the right of the fairway, 10 yards or so from the rough.

The second shot was one of those strong-back-weak-mind tragedies that so frequently happen to the ordinary golfer. Bill threw all of his poundage but very little of the clubhead into the shot. I hadn't said a word to him before he walked up to make that shot. It was a simple space shot. He had 330 yards to go to the hole and acres of unmarred fairway to the left. It would have been perfectly obvious to a ten-year-old boy that as long as the green couldn't be reached by one shot, two easy shots should be played.

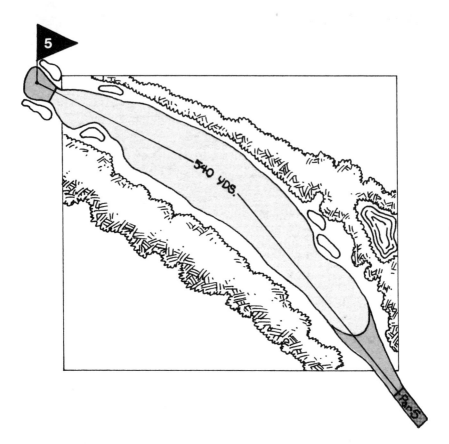

Bill's frantic lunge moved the ball only a little more than one hundred yards diagonally across the fairway.

We both looked in sickened silence at the shot. I knew the man's soul was bleeding. What had happened was that almost everything went wrong with his swing. He fell back instead of turning his body and shoulders. He didn't get his feet in position to transfer weight onto his left foot and begin the downswing after he'd lifted the club up.

His grip was so tight his knuckles were white. His right elbow flew away from his side. He stiffened out his arms and wrists at the top of the swing and fell at the ball instead of swinging at it.

There were other errors, too, but I didn't want to rebuke Bill by detailing mistakes. In the first place the catalogue of errors was too long to recite and, secondly, it's much easier and more effective to point out something that the fellow should do right instead of keeping him bleeding with memories of what he did wrong.

I can tell you, though, one little but tremendously important thing that, about nine out of ten times, will prevent the casualty of a shot missed as badly as Bill had missed his second shot.

My tip simply is to pause a wee moment at the top of the backswing. It is miraculous what instinctive correction can occur during that hesitation. Instead of lurching at the ball you will give yourself an instant in which you can steady yourself and regain some command of the club with your hands.

All I could hope for at this time was that Bill would not butcher another shot by trying too hard with everything but his brain. I relaxed him with a little talk about the pause of the hands at the top of the swing.

The cooling-off period seemed to help him. He stood up to the next shot without showing any signs of being tight.

He might have reached one of the bunkers near the green with an exceptional shot but instead he played with a 4-wood and didn't strain for distance. He hit the ball about 180 yards, a little less than 40 yards from the green.

The next shot he had to play was one that separates the men from the boys. The preceding shot had been one of those easy, satisfying ones that erase bitter recollections. By now Bill was believing that he'd played all the holes all by himself and that only the demands of his business kept him from going out after big championships.

He grabbed a 9-iron. It was the proper club. The green to

which he was playing had a few mild undulations but generally was rather flat. What he needed to do was to pitch at the hole rather than play a chip shot that might bump into a small knob and slide far off the line.

Bill bent over the ball with his feet wide apart. His posture was fine for sweeping a ball with a short-handled broom but not for hitting a ball with a golf club.

He was getting excited and in a hurry to get the ball into the hole. He was hoping, not thinking.

His grip was O.K. That was about all that was right. His heels were nearly three feet apart. He was standing somewhat pigeon-toed and his weight was on his toes. The ball was in line with his left toe and he was leaning to the right.

Should I let him try to play the shot from that atrocious address or direct him to the proper procedure?

I couldn't stand looking at him on the brink of disaster.

"Don't do that to me!" I implored.

Bill straightened up and looked at me, puzzled. "What do you mean?"

"I mean that you ought to think about what you are supposed to do."

"Tommy, don't worry. I'll make this one."

"You probably won't. Why don't you try to play it correctly, even if you miss it? The odds are better for you when you try to make the shot as it should be made. You can half-top the shot the way you're going at it and maybe have the ball skim along pretty well toward the hole four times out of ten, but when you play the shot right you'll get satisfactory results ten times out of ten."

"What's wrong with the way I'm going at it?" asked Bill.

"Never mind what's wrong. Get thinking about what's right. First of all, get your feet close together. You don't need any footwork and body action in this shot. Merely have your feet and body free from tension. Stand up as close to the ball as you are allowed to by the length of the shaft and the lie of that club when you've soled it behind the ball. Open your stance. Have your toes about on a 45-degree angle from the line to the hole so your body will be faced around toward the hole."

Bill adjusted his stance.

"Play the ball off your right toe. You'll notice your left arm and the shaft of the club are in a line from your shoulder joint to the clubface. You are leaning just the least little bit to the left because your weight is mainly on your left foot and it should stay there all through the shot.

"Remember to keep your head steady, swing smoothly with your shoulders, and slap the ball smartly with your hands. It is much simpler than it sounds. Most of it you do in getting ready to shoot. Let's try it."

Bill stepped away from the ball and made a practice swing.

"Take the club straight back. Get into your head the general idea of knocking the ball into the ground; not knocking the ground into the ball. The duffer makes a scoop at these shots. The golfer hits them," I told Bill. "Now go ahead and shoot."

Bill looked good as he addressed the ball. He took the club back well — then everything must have gone blank. He staggered into the ball and shanked it wretchedly into the bunker.

He stared at me with the horror-stricken gaze of a man who'd just shanked.

He got no sympathy from me. He stood there with his nerves raw and the ball lying in the sand like a bleached skull along the old Santa Fe Trail.

"Can I try it again?" he entreated.

"No!"

"What went wrong?"

"Think about that and you'll do it wrong again. Remember the main idea — stay still and hit with your hands. You misplayed another shot by trying to hit with your body instead of your hands."

"Well, I'll do it right this time."

"There won't be another time here. You haven't been able to stand concentration yet, but you'll learn if I have to pound it into you. You've got to concentrate, think and do right the first time. A cow could hit the ball right the second time. You're not going to be encouraged to be sloppy and get two chances to think."

Bill stalked off toward the bunker.

"Play the same shot you splashed out of the bunker on the hole before. Open up the club and go through with the shot," I reminded Bill.

He walked up to the shot, wriggled his feet to get a good foundation in the sand and played a perfect shot. The ball skidded and stopped about six feet from the pin.

Bill looked over the line of the putt from back of the ball to the hole, then from beyond the hole back to the ball.

"Am I right? Let it drop in from the left-hand edge?" he asked.

"You are. And if you miss it on the right-hand side we'll call the whole deal off and walk right into the clubhouse." I wanted to put some hard pressure on Bill. If a golfer is under pressure and can analyze the situation and perform smoothly his brain is functioning, but if he gets into a critical spot and becomes jerky and almost paralyzed he's hopeless. He beats himself.

My partner took a couple of practice strokes with his putter to get the feel, then stepped up to the ball apparently with a clear picture of the putt in his mind. That clarity always gives a man confidence.

And what do you think happened?

He holed his putt!

It curved just enough toward the end to drop into the hole without any trembling.

The trembling was done by Bill after the putt was holed and the pressure was off.

We got off the green and I gave him the box score on brain and brawn for the fifth hole.

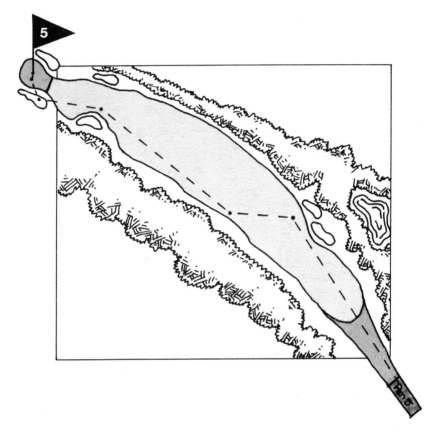

How Bill played the fifth hole

"Your drive was an admirable exhibition of balanced mental and physical action. Your head figured out what should be done and allowed your muscles to do it. A peculiar thing about golf as it is often played by average golfers is that they actually spend a lot of effort in preventing the correct and easy action.

"Your second shot was a lugubrious affair. You charged at the ball blindly like an infuriated water buffalo. The shot was perfect in one way — it was perfectly brainless.

"The third shot was hit efficiently. You applied the required amount of effort and got maximum results. You didn't need one ounce more of force for that distance. The clubhead was traveling at top speed when it hit the ball. You kept your body steady so your arms and hands operated in ideal leverage. Your coordination was such that everything was geared correctly together at the right time.

"There were more fine things in that shot than are dreamt of in your philosophy — and in mine, too, I will admit — and most of them were simply allowed to occur as the natural result of a correct start and a normal development, instead of being forced."

"Do you mean that all you have to do is to begin a shot right, then don't interfere with its natural progress?" Bill wondered out loud.

"It's not that simple, but if you know what the natural progress should be you can think so you will promote it. Your shank was a case of forcing a mistake. You tried to steer that shot instead of being content to hit it simply and squarely. You pushed yourself at the ball and your club was coming from so far outside the line of flight that only the shank of the club and not the clubface could get against the ball.

"But don't be downcast. Your shot out of the bunker and that putt of yours both showed head. You have the rigorous task of breaking some bad habits. Your worst habit is that of not thinking out a specific and direct plan of procedure. You've got to train yourself to determine what shot is to be made, then execute it."

Bill remarked, "When I hit one I hit it good, don't I?"

"You do. Most golfers of your kind hit a number of shots about as well as almost any professional can hit them; maybe not as far, but far enough. To make those shots, you follow a logical routine, accidentally or deliberately. But when you go at a shot haphazardly, as you do most of the time, the percentage is against you. You haven't the conditioned reflexes of a fellow who has practiced and played a lot, so you must go at the job thinking carefully."

The other fellows were waiting for us on the sixth tee. We stepped up our gait.

*B*efore I tell you about playing the sixth hole I want to attend to a matter that I'd noticed while watching my amateur pals exhibit the range of their merits and deficiencies.

None of the three had a really first-grade stance as uniform procedure. Mainly by accident they were able to start swinging correctly.

As I looked at them I recalled another one of the sessions at which Ty Cobb and I had compared baseball and golf.

We had talked about developing a uniform swing and had agreed that wonders can be worked in improving hitting of the baseball and of the golf ball by making slight alterations in the stance.

Bill needed to think about his stance. He wasn't aware of it but he was making the game very difficult by changing his stance in some little (or big) way almost every shot.

On some shots he would be bent over so much and holding his head so low that he'd have to look up shortly after he'd started swinging.

On other shots he'd be stiff-kneed and as upright as a guardsman at review. My other two companions were inclined to be a bit more at ease but at times crouched too much.

In talking with Cobb (and Stan Musial, too) about batting I'd been told by both of them that the first thing a batter does after the pitcher delivers the ball is to spring up out of the crouch. In baseball the crouch is a decoy. It may help to deceive the pitcher.

In baseball you get three swings at the ball. In golf you get only one and that is at a ball that doesn't move, so it gives you time to straighten up out of your crouch.

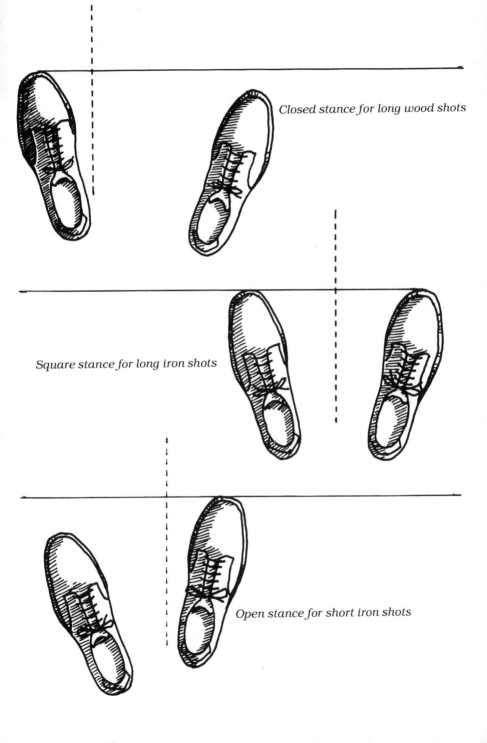

Closed stance for long wood shots

Square stance for long iron shots

Open stance for short iron shots

The fellows against whom Bill and I were playing suggested in their stances the crouch of a football player who is making ready to throw a block. That doesn't fit golf at all. In golf the body must stay in the same place and act as the fulcrum of all the leverage in the swing.

Golf is played standing up, not lying down or leaning.

Clubs are designed so if they are correctly fitted to you they will measure the distance you should stand from the ball when you're addressing it. Your arms should hang down with your hands close enough to your body so you feel that you are in easy, steady balance, and when you sole the club so it is flat on the ground behind the ball there isn't the slightest sensation of reaching out for the ball.

Your knees must be unlocked so they can turn easily. They will be bent and loose enough when you push your hind end back a little bit and have the center of balance running up about in line with the arches of your feet to just below your shoulders.

Your right shoulder is quite a little lower than your left shoulder at address because of your right hand being lower on the grip of the club and because the right elbow is loose and bent a bit so it is fairly close to your right hip.

Your left arm should feel a trifle stretched at address, but it must not be rigid. It shouldn't be measuring the radius of the swing.

Whether you stand at address with your head cocked a little bit to the right or with your chin straight down is pretty much up to you. Some believe that having the head turned to the right slightly makes it easier for the left shoulder to slide under the chin in the backswing. If thoughtful experimentation and practice show that this turn of the chin helps you to make a body turn instead of swaying, then cock your head as standard procedure. What you are seeking is free shoulder action and a steady head.

In the final analysis, if your head doesn't move your body

doesn't sway and you maintain a stable axis for your swing. But you don't have to keep your head as still as a statue. It probably will bob up and down a little as you shift weight and it may turn a mite as you swing back, then recover its original position as you get set to hit, but there won't be any conspicuous movement of your head.

There are two factors to have in mind as you stand to the ball. One is the position of your feet with relation to the ball. The other is your position for maintaining balance while you are turning your body, swinging your arms and whipping your hands in generating and delivering power.

In a general way Bill knew about addressing the ball. But he didn't know just how to use this knowledge in preparing for the uniform execution of shots.

He didn't understand that the position of the ball in relation to his feet determined at what point in the arc of his swing the ball would be hit. If the ball was about in line with his left heel he'd probably be hitting the ball exactly at the bottom of the arc or even when the clubface was on its way up. Logically, then, that would be the right place for the ball when using a straight-faced club, the driver. At that point the ball should be teed up well.

As the stance is moved to the left and the ball is played closer to a line extending from the right toe, the arc of the swing reaches the lowest point ahead of the ball.

Bill also didn't make intelligent use of the simple principles of the stances: the open stance when there is to be very little body movement in the stroke; the square stance when the swing is to be more upright than the player's swing for the drive and other long wood shots; and the closed stance when the body is to turn fully and the club is to be thrown from inside to out and give the ball a long traveling hook spin.

If Bill ever did know he needed to be reminded again that his toes, especially his left toes, should be turned outward at address for the medium and longer shots. That allows more body turning with less strain on the back. Some advocate having the right foot at a right angle to the line of flight, but I advise that only for the short shots where there is to be very little, or no body action.

I suggested to Bill that he put a bit more weight on his right foot than on his left when addressing his drive, so he'd be able to get a good smooth start in transferring weight and moving around on his backswing. That feeling of stability on the right foot and the rebound from a forward press help to fling the club around and up in an even, flowing way.

Another thing I mentioned to Bill that helped him was to loosen his shoulders. Stiff, cramped shoulders at address are one of the most common indications of nervousness and uncertainty that the average golfer shows.

Although the plan of our play together didn't call for any throwback to instruction in the essentials of shotmaking, I snapped Bill into the habit of thinking about the ABCs. The grip was *A* and the stance was *B*.

I found that one reason he'd been so discouraged was because he topped many of his shots. Until I told him what was ailing him, he was bent over so far that he simply had to straighten up and top the ball. If he'd tried to stay bent over the way he was at address he wouldn't have been able to keep his footing while he was swinging.

11

A Deceptive Hole and the Solution to Its Puzzles
(The Sixth Hole)

*F*amous golfers have talked of our sixth as one of the greatest short par-4 holes in the world.

It is 340 yards long and I could tell you 340 tales about the various ways it has been played. It is a storybook hole that tests ability and concentration. In championships noted golfers have found it a fearful experience. It beckons as a siren beguiles, then wrecks the unwary. Many a seasoned contestant has stood on this sixth tee dreaming of a birdie and has awakened, after a nightmare, to write a horrendous 8 or a fatal 11 on a card.

The fairway is narrow. The green is what usually is termed kidney-shaped. However, the outlining curves of the green are so voluptuous you don't feel like being clinical and referring to kidneys.

There is a deep bunker in front and to the right. If you are not prudent and proficient this bunker may jump up and chew up your prospect for a decent score.

This is one of those rare holes showing brilliant architecture. It doesn't depend on distance over expensive real estate to make it a hole that will only test the strength of the long-hitter. There are too many holes of that dull and extravagant sort. The member who pays dues and the tournament player who makes money by playing a course both find our Number Six hole fair but mighty tough.

It's a hole that makes all smart men equal, something like Samuel Colt's contribution to the arsenal of small arms.

The hole is so tight that par 4 practically is a birdie and a 5 is a score you can accept with relief. Only a few 3s are registered here during a season.

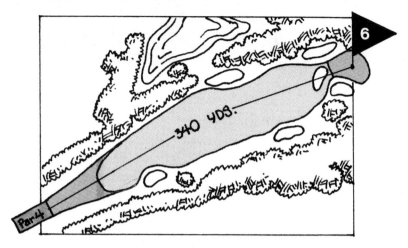

The entrance to the green is from the left and you've got to play two perfect shots to get onto the green and stay on.

I said to Bill, "I am glad that this hole is your deal alone. It has made me respect it. It is going to determine how well you can think golf and how well you can play golf."

Bill laughed. "So the pressure is on me?"

"What pressure? Your life doesn't go with it. You will play this hole in your best, worst or in-between manner and still be able to go home and eat a hearty dinner tonight. But if you play it well you will have a thrill that will give you good appetite and good digestion and win you the right to look into the eyes of your fellow men and call yourself a golfer."

I sat on the tee bench making that oration as Bill looked over the terrain trying to decide where to tee his ball.

To guide his thinking I remarked, "There's only one question: How are you going to attack this hole? By the card it is a simple 4; by construction it can be a difficult 8. Using a few of your millions of brain cells I can maneuver the ball into the hole in five strokes."

Bill replied, "Maybe you can. But I'm playing this one all alone."

He was sweating a little when he teed the ball. He placed the ball properly on the right side of the tee. The tee shot had to be to the left because of the entrance to the hole and to take advantage of the long dimension of the green.

Bill was really getting good at the tee shots. By teeing the ball so he could let his club fly and have a big landing area for his drive he wouldn't have to try to steer the shot. That protected him against stiffening.

He got a nice, firm, flexible grip. He stayed down to the shot so his right shoulder went well under his chin before he turned his head. He stayed back of the ball, threw his right hand into the shot like a third baseman lining one across to first, and kept the club in the groove adroitly with his left hand.

It was one of those shots that healed the wounds of some sorry efforts. Our opponents and I looked at Bill's drive in admiration. It went a good 220 yards to the left, just exactly where perfect play for a golfer like Bill called for a drive.

He was 120 yards from the hole. The pin was placed behind the bunker and not with any too much room between the sand and the cup.

Bill could go directly for the pin but if he didn't hit the shot exactly right he'd be in bad shape. If he went over the green he'd be down in a wooded hollow that we call Death Valley. If he went short and a little off line he'd be in abysmal bunkers. The left bunker isn't the terror that the right one is because you can come out of the left bunker playing the long axis of the green, but even so, you've got to play a first-class wedge shot to get out of that pit and stay on the green.

I put the situation up to Bill so he'd use imagination in making his campaign and asked, "If you were playing for big money what would you do now? What club would you use?"

"But we're not playing for big money. We're only playing for fun. You are doing all right for me. We're ahead at this stage," my partner responded.

I shook my head. "Maybe you're only playing for fun, but I'm not. This is serious business for me. I am devoting my time and experience to showing how an average golfer can get around a golf course much better than he usually does. The other fellows are being slowed up but seem to find the deal interesting. No, sir, my friend, this is not for fun. You are studying for your degree, so get that brain of yours busy."

To my astonishment, and that of the other fellows and the caddies, Bill took out an 8-iron. We didn't think he'd be conservative.

When I looked at him inquiringly he explained, "I'm going to play this to the left of the line to the hole. I've got the safe line in my mind and I'm not going to look at the pin."

He took his stance and waggled his club a few times, then stepped away from the ball.

"What's wrong?" I asked.

He replied, "I don't know. I just don't feel right."

He was using his head this time. I have been criticized for not stepping right up to the shot and taking a bang at it. I've heard Middlecoff and Hogan censured by gallery experts who shoot 90 when they're lucky, because Middlecoff and Hogan take time with shots. But the valuable truth is that you save time in golf by taking enough time to feel right before you begin to swing.

Bill finally got himself settled and appeared to be in stable balance and free enough to be able to swing smoothly.

Again he'd had the ball at the right spot in relation to his feet and again he stayed down to the ball and swung rather lazily until his hands punched into the shot.

The ball, as it does on shots when a golfer thinks about nothing except hitting with precision, authority and no haste, was better than Bill knew how to make.

It soared onto the green, took a couple of hops and coasted to a halt about thirty feet to the left of the hole.

The rest was an anticlimax. He made two good putts. The first one he rolled to about two feet away from the hole. It wasn't on the high side and I didn't regard that as a mistake because the green sloped quite abruptly around the hole. The smart thing to do was to lag up safely so if a long and lucky putt wasn't holed, the next putt would be one of those short uphill putts that make the hole look nine feet wide.

I wish I could describe what he did in handling the thirty-foot putt so well. The job was almost wholly a matter of touch and how can you describe touch?

Touch is something that has the fingertips doing the talking. I suppose that someday somebody could write a learned treatise on the ulnar and digital nerves that might help explain the feeling of a good putt, but after you'd get through reading it you would forget to hit the ball.

I've tried a million ways — more or less — to get the correct sensation of touch over to pupils of mine. In those efforts I have used similes that I thought were keyed to the personality of the golf pupil so there'd be a vivid mental picture painted, but the sensation of the correct touch in golf completely baffles analysis and description. About all I know for sure about touch that might do you any good is to say that sensitive touch is in your fingertips and if you press hard the sensitivity will be deadened.

When you learn the feel of a fine golf shot — and it is a combination, I suppose, of sensations originating in various areas of your system — you know what should be done to play good golf, but you won't know the words to tell exactly how to recapture the feeling.

What had happened to Bill on the green at the sixth hole was that he was so relaxed after getting to the green in two fine shots that his nerves and muscles were loose and delicately responsive. Hence the two fine putts.

He didn't realize it then but he had added another story to my library of sixth-hole tales. He was the colorless common golfer who had played the hole absolutely perfectly.

When we left the green I thought of a couple of highly proficient professionals who probably would have won a couple of national championships if they had played this hole as well as it had just been played by a high-handicap golfer unknown to glory.

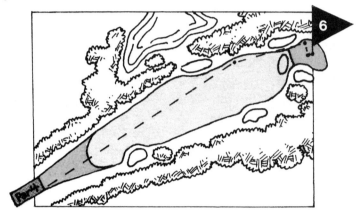

How Bill played the sixth hole

12

*T*here isn't much that you can say about a 130-yard water hole except that there are enough balls dumped into the water every year to pay the dues and house accounts of three very active members.

Our seventh is just 130 yards from the tee to the middle of the cup and most of that yardage is across water. It is the same kind of water there is on all other inland water holes. At Indian Creek in Florida and at Cypress Point and Pebble Beach in California, there are exciting water holes with salt water, and on inland courses there are a few shots on par-3 holes across fresh water that merit praise, but most water holes are merely holes with water as a substitute for turf. The substitution is nothing by itself to identify a hole as an example of golf architectural genius.

The only thing that distinguishes most water holes is that if you don't hit the ball fairly well you are in the water and if you do hit the ball halfway decently you are on the green.

After looking at many water holes from a psychological viewpoint I've come to the conclusion that the holes are so inferior they cause the golfer to feel inferior.

The average player plays an old ball at a water hole. At least, you may be sure that he's not going to tear the wrapping off a brand-new ball and tee it up at a water hole.

The instant the fellow picks out the old ball and tees it he is licked, psychologically. He is saying to himself, subconsciously, "I'm going to fluff this one into the water."

And that's exactly what Bill started to do to beat himself before he really began to play the hole.

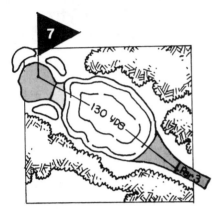

He dug into the ball pocket of his bag and hauled out a ball that looked as though it had been played thirty-six holes with an ax.

"Not this time, buddy," I called. "I'm playing this hole for you. Get out a new ball and tee it up."

"Pardon me, I forgot that you are also in the golf ball business," said Bill, smiling. He made a flourish at the pond. "A pretty hole for the professionals, isn't it? Dotted with lilies decorating the graves of thousands of golf balls."

"Now that you've held services, how about attending to this shot? Let's compare plans," I suggested.

He got serious and seemed to be studying the hole. "I'm going to play it safe," he concluded and took out a 4-wood.

I winced. Bill had gone too far in taking advice about caution. I stopped him.

"Oh, no. If you hit the shot truly with that club you'll go forty yards over the green and if you try to play the shot soft it's twenty-five to one that you'll plop it into the pond!"

Bill looked at the glistening white ball he'd teed and wanted to argue.

"With a 4-wood I'll hit it so I'm bound to get over, and even if I do get way past the green I can get back on in one stroke and down in one or two."

"That's possible," I admitted, "but you will miss the beauty of playing a simple section of woodland scenery correctly and you will destroy your morale."

"My morale? What do you mean, my morale?" Bill asked.

"I mean your capacity to look at the facts, put them in order, and keep from being panicked. Now let's analyze what has happened so far at this hole. Every thought you've had, every move you've made, has been the result of more concern about the possibility of losing a ball than thinking about hitting the ball close to the hole.

"The hole requires from you a good shot with a 5- or 6-iron, so you do everything expecting a bad shot. You sell yourself on the idea that you can't get over the water. You stand there and look at a tiny pool until it grows in your mind to the extent that it's bigger than the Atlantic. Instead of seeing a nice big green that is an easy shot ahead, you see the Loch Ness monster sticking its slimy head up, leering at you and demanding that it feed it golf balls," I said to Bill.

"Tommy, you are a mind reader," Bill chuckled. "Why should I come to this hole scared as a kid having to walk through a graveyard at midnight? Every time I get here I am so confident that I'll get a bad shot I seldom disappoint myself."

"This time you are going to shake the curse," I promised. "We want no pusillanimous effort here. You are going to slam this up to that pin. Go at the shot like a man. You won't be taken off the field on your shield like a fallen gladiator if you do miss the green, so go it."

When Bill was led into appreciating that a 130-yard shot over water doesn't differ at all from a 130-yard shot over grass and is made with the same club and the same swing, he began to think clearly and constructively about hitting the ball.

He stood with the ball about halfway between his feet — maybe an inch or so nearer his right foot — and he hit down at the ball instead of making the ordinary golfer's frequent mistake of trying to lift the shot. When they do that they're almost certain to fall back on the right leg and top the ball into the water.

Bill's shot went beautifully about thirty feet beyond and to the left, above the hole.

I advised him to try to figure out a way to allow for a margin of error on the low side where he could stroke the putt positively instead of trying to trickle it into the cup.

He almost holed the putt. It curved off short and below the cup. I'd urge him to stroke through with his putter even if the putt was downhill. So many fellows get scared and make a jerky tap at a long downhill putt, and they don't get any touch at all to the stroke.

There was a little sidehill borrow on the putt of a couple of feet that Bill had left and he was looking that borrow over inch by inch.

"Forget the dainty business," I said. "Remember what I told you on the fourth green. Hit the ball firmly and with the sweet spot of your putter right at the center of the cup. There may be such a thing as a borrow on a short putt but never anywhere near as much as you think there is, so don't try to nurse the putt along a curved line, figuring on the pull of gravity. If you do you make the putt too difficult. Go at the short putt steadily like a surgeon operating.

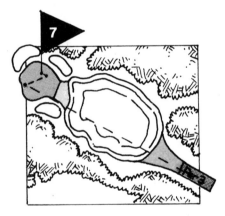

How Bill played the seventh hole

"The greatest I ever saw at short putts was Johnny Revolta. Johnny walked up to a short putt as though he were saying to himself, 'To hell with the line,' and smashed the ball into the hole.

"I might add that after being a victim of Revolta's superb technique on short putts, a method that didn't allow the ball to have any doubt about going into the hole, I copied the process. I didn't get as uniformly successful at it as Johnny, but I did learn that the system eliminated twists that I had thought existed on the green between the ball and the hole.

"You'll learn the same thing I did when you tap those short putts squarely at the center of the cup. Now go do it."

He did.

*A*s Bill and I walked from the seventh green to the eighth tee I mentioned to him that we were engaged in a paradoxical venture; we were working to make golf more fun. There was immediately ahead of him an exacting period of mental effort as our eighth hole is a long par 4, a dog-leg from left to right. It has big bunkers flanking its fairway and this day a stiff wind blew into our faces as we looked toward the green.

With the wind pushing at us the hole for Bill and our opposition was one that probably couldn't be reached by two good shots. Bill could make it in three easy shots if he played correctly.

The tee is wide. Bill walked to the right side of the tee, bent over to stick his peg into the turf, then straightened up.

"I'd better hit this one from the left side and let it fly out with plenty of room," he remarked. He was right. If he played the ball from the left side of the tee the matter of landing area for his drive could be dismissed from his mind. All he'd have to think of was how to hit the shot. And when you are thinking only of hitting the shot you'll probably send it flying out satisfactorily far and straight.

This is no hole for straying to the right. On the right are dense trees close to the fairway and the fairway slopes toward that border of forest.

You could almost feel Bill's concentration working. He picked his direction line and aimed his feet, body and shoulders correctly. He waggled the club a few times, then stepped away from the ball.

"I don't feel just right yet," he explained.

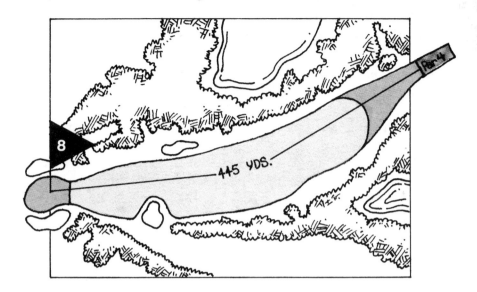

Stepping away when you know you are unbalanced and awkward is always the proper thing to do. You'd better begin your stance all over again. Then you've got a good chance of standing correctly to the ball — not too stiff and not too sloppy, but in good balance and in good muscular tone.

When he got back to the ball feeling loose, but not too loose, he swung smoothly, lashed the club into the ball, and let the force of his follow-through turn him around nicely.

The shot was another one of his top-grade drives. It did Bill a great deal of good not to have to worry about steering a drive so it stayed out of trouble.

"How was that?" he asked with justifiable pride. I felt proud of him, too.

"A grand shot," I congratulated him, then warned, "but you've still got a long way to go."

The rest of the route was not only long, it was dangerous. The fairway bent to the right and toward the green. The second shot had to stay away from a yawning bunker that was about 100 yards out from the green and on the left of the fairway.

That left-hand bunker was deceitful. It was located where it had Bill overestimating the length of his drive although he was fully aware that a fairly stiff wind blowing at him had cut down the distance of his tee shots. He stood at the ball apparently planning to carry the bunker. There wouldn't be anything to be gained by hitting a ball over that bunker but I imagined that Bill had made the shot once or twice and felt like showing us that he could do it again.

However, he wisely second-guessed after looking over the prospects and figured that a sidehill lie with him standing above the ball was going to be a problem that he had better handle with care.

That sort of a shot will fade 90 per cent of the times it's made. You are standing so you can't turn as easily as you can on level ground and you have to make an upright swing.

Bill took his 3-wood and aimed to the right of the bunker. He made another fine swing. It was obvious that he had set up a plan in his mind and was going to trust his swing.

The shot had more fade to it than Bill had anticipated. It landed in the rough but it wasn't lying too badly. On most courses these days the rough isn't much more than long fairway. The game has been softened a lot by elimination of the tough and tight rough that bordered most fairways until about a dozen years ago.

My companion plainly was proud of his technique and judgment as he walked up to his ball. He appraised the situation and lifted a 9-iron out of his bag.

He was beginning to give me hope that he was learning fast and escaping from the terrors that arise in the imagination of the average golfer. Right here was one of those short shots that the ordinary player fears might go into a bunker guarding a green, so he doesn't concentrate on hitting the ball. He tries to scoop it up and he falls back onto his right foot. Up comes the club with its sole nipping the ball above its middle and skidding it along the grass.

Bill's shot, sliced, landing in rough

Take a slightly open stance

*Ball played a bit farther back
from a line off the left heel —
weight slightly more on left foot*

*There is a tendency to slice,
so take a club one or two
stronger than usual. Aim to left
of pin because of probability
of slice.*

Downhill lie in the fairway

But Bill played this one as it should be played. He took an open stance with the ball off the right foot and his weight accented on his left foot. When you do this and keep the left arm straight as you're swinging, the wrists hinge pretty much automatically.

Something else that Bill did right was hitting down at the ball so the loft of the clubface could smack the ball up. He also made the club go through the shot and toward the flag. The ordinary hacker digs into the ground behind the ball and stops hitting. There is hope but no purpose to that sort of a shot.

Bill's shot was quite an achievement. If he'd missed it the error would have been caused by one of those mysterious frailties of man for which there is no accounting. But the procedure in this case was as perfect as one could expect. The ball went about twenty-five feet past the hole. A shot like that going boldly past the hole is intelligently played. It has been given a chance.

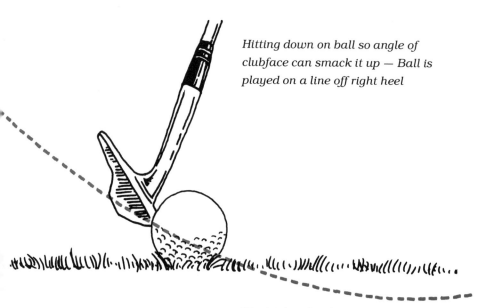

Hitting down on ball so angle of clubface can smack it up — Ball is played on a line off right heel

Divot taken by shot

Let me repeat something I've said and written many times for the benefit of 98 per cent of golfers: Don't worry about putting stop on approach shots but think about hitting them up to or past the hole.

Usually golfers forget that the high trajectory of shots made with the short clubs will cut down distance. On shots made with 8- or 9-irons or wedges you'd better shoot for the flag rather than for the hole.

If Bill had played this approach from a fairway lie he'd probably have had enough backspin on the ball to have it bite and stay close to the hole. The longer grass of the rough got between the clubface and the ball in this shot, hence the application of backspin was impossible.

Bill was assimilating principles of how to play golf as well as applying the principles of properly hitting the ball.

He lined up his putt, figured the slope wisely, and made a flowing stroke without his head or body moving. The ball stopped only a couple of inches away and on the proper side of the hole. He tapped that short one in and glowed with satisfaction as he straightened up with the ball in his hand.

"I'll make no complaints about picking up that 5; the champions don't do it so much better," he boasted.

"Comparatively, you played the hole better than many experts," I told him. "That hole, with the wind against you, is a par 5 for your kind of golfer. Now do you know how you got it or was it just a case of heaven helping you five times in succession?"

Bill vehemently declared, "Certainly I know how I got that par. I played five perfectly hit shots."

I put my hand on his shoulder. "Take it easy, champ. And let me tell you you've confirmed what I suspected. You've still got a lot to learn, so in your moment of glory don't lose sight of the main objectives."

"Which are?" asked Bill.

"First, to hit fewer bad shots and, second, to learn to use

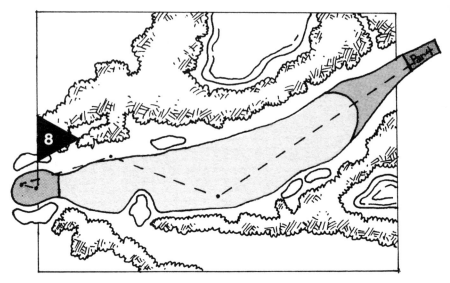

How Bill played the eighth hole

correctly the shots that you do know how to play. Both purposes are more matters of mentality than they are of muscle. I would say that you probably have as much brain capacity as the greatest golfers — maybe more — but you still haven't much of an idea how to employ your brains in playing golf."

I've heard that old line about one not having to be stupid to be able to play good golf but being stupid helps. The crack is not a gem of intellectual observation. What is meant, possibly, is that the fellow who can shut out distracting thoughts and make the shot rather mechanically, using about the same brain power he'd use to scratch himself, enjoys an advantage over the fellow with an active mind and lively imagination. Perhaps that is true up to a certain point, but I doubt it. I don't think that a fellow of that type could truly enjoy golf.

For years I have been seeing 75-shooting professionals and amateurs who know how to hit the ball but who don't know much more about how to play golf than I know about atomic fission. Any unusual problem of tactics or competitive pressure defeats these fellows who are solely mechanics at the game.

Times without number I have seen young men on practice tees — tournament circuit contestants — who can hit shots as well as any golfer I've ever seen but who can't pass the rigorous tests of playing. I also have seen older and more notable golfers who have failed in critical situations, not really because of luck being against them, but because of lack of mental keenness or discipline required in the fell clutch of circumstance.

Most of the 75s that I have looked at (including my own) have included at least three shots, and generally five, that were absolutely thrown away by thinking wrong or by not thinking.

I never have objected to a bad shot that was caused by failure to achieve the delicate mechanical precision necessary in golf, but what does burn me is the brainless shot.

The brainless shot is the one unforgivable sin in golf, and a diabolical thing about it is that so many times it is made by men who, off a golf course, are mentally superior.

14 THE LONG WAY BACK THE EASY WAY (The Ninth Hole)

By the time Bill and I got to the ninth tee we were showing the strain.

I'd been carrying the thinking responsibilities on the odd holes and Bill had enjoyed a mental recess then. On the even holes where Bill was supposed to think for himself I continued to examine and apply remedies to the mental part of the play, so I didn't get any letup. Furthermore, I had to provide Bill and the other boys with a good example and didn't dare allow myself any lapses in concentration.

Nobody can convince me that lifting a fourteen-ounce club is work or that a well-conditioned athlete can tire himself by walking four miles or so on the pleasant turf of a golf course.

But I've heard boxers and wrestlers say that they have felt wearier after playing a close golf match with a pal than after strenuous performances in their own professional sports.

Again, I suggest as evidence of golf's tension, the drawn faces of golf championship winners. Compare their appearance with that of other athletes photographed right after victory. That will give you an idea of what golf's demand for repeated and intense concentration takes out of a fellow.

I didn't want Bill to take golf brutally hard but I did want him to learn to play golf with an active and educated mind instead of merely walking around and pounding a stick at a ball senselessly.

Inwardly I was feeling ready to quit but I didn't dare let Bill know. I was out of training on concentration, to tell the truth, and was finding that I'd been depending too much on long-established good habits in analyzing a situation and playing a shot.

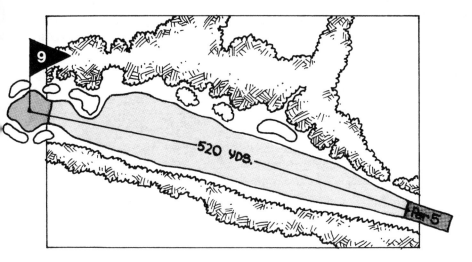

Concentration is a fatiguing business when you're not accustomed to it. Concentrating on writing this book and thumbing the dictionary for a word that will get across the picture I want to put in your head is hard work for me. After a morning at this task an afternoon playing a rugged golf course is fun and delightful refreshment.

Without being conscious of it I'd possibly been a bit too sharp with Bill. That hadn't made things easier for either one of us but we both were lucky in understanding each other. Bill realized that he represented a challenge to my pride in showing myself and him that I was able to teach him how to play better golf. I felt that Bill, like so many other very successful businessmen, had been pampered at his golf. He hadn't been taught sternly, so he would be encouraged to learn something by himself. Instead he had fallen into the custom of depending on a professional who had been attempting the impossible job of nursing him into command of a first-class game.

From being a fellow who'd wanted to quit the game and who had to be almost shanghaied to the first tee, Bill had become cocky and avid. His cheering performances on the sixth and eighth holes had given golf a new look to him.

Here at the ninth tee he stood like stout Cortez with eagle eyes as he stared at a 520-yard hole. The wind was pushing into him. With distance, wind, a narrow fairway bordered by bunkers on the right, and a green tightly trapped, all united against him, Bill began to realize that he was up for a harsh examination. He shook his head.

"What do you think about this one, Tommy?"

"It's your turn to think. You've played two fine holes out of eight so far, now see if you can play two consecutively."

"Yeah, but this is the toughest par 5 on the course."

"I know it. I can read the distances on the card."

"The fifth is a bit longer. But look at those bunkers. They don't show on the card but my clubs can see them."

"The only help I'll give you right now is to mention to you that at long holes it has been the habit of boobs for centuries to hit the ball hard, and for the same centuries and at the same long holes the experts have hit the ball easy. I can tell you from my own experience that I have made a considerable amount of money and won a collection of important championships by hitting the ball easy. Now, off with you into the wild blue yonder."

Bill studied the layout to get an idea of the target that he could reach with the least risk and the best percentage of probable performance. Obviously he was having trouble making up his mind what to do.

I couldn't stand the suspense. "Stay away from trouble and remember that as long as it looks you can reach it with three easy 4-wood shots. If I direct you any more and you get a par 5 here you won't feel as though you had achieved it independently. So get to work all by yourself. If you don't want to do that, why don't you pick up the ball and walk in?"

Then Bill stepped up to the ball, waggling his club. His grip looked good and appeared to be loose enough so he could get a lot of spring from his hands into the shot. He teed the ball wisely, a bit lower than for a drive in which oncoming wind wasn't a factor.

At that point he very plainly began to freeze.

A fellow can learn from suffering but he doesn't want to invite that education, and after trouble is over and the scar is healed a man may be able to say "Sweet are the uses of adversity" and mean it. But not one breath of that philosophy would score with Bill as he viewed the ninth. He had suffered too many 7s, 8s, and 9s on that hole to have any desire to submit to another beating there, instinctively or not.

He shuddered in a manner that I imagine he hoped would be a forward press and at that moment I cried to him, "Hold it!

Bill jerked his swing to a halt, then turned to me in relief.

"What did you stop me for?"

"Because I didn't want you to tear yourself apart, hitting the ball 340 yards. The ball wouldn't have gone that far. You'd have hit it about 140 yards to the right or hammered it right on top. But you would have wrenched every muscle in your body and have done practically nothing to the ball. Now, go to it again and swing moderately. And when you get well along in your downswing and ought to begin hitting, in the name of St. Andrew, hit! Throw both your hands into the hit and do it as fiercely as you know how. But up to that point, take it easy. The easier you hit this ball the farther it's going to go."

Bill listened studiously.

He went back to the ball and took his stance, thinking about his swing rather than about the narrowness of the fairway and the length of the hole. He'd just hurdled a mental block.

He turned in an excellent, smooth swing. He almost seemed to be relaxed and that's an extraordinary thing for an average golfer who is hitting a shot into the wind. Usually they are grim and inflexible.

His hand action at the bottom of the swing was fast. When

you don't hurry to whip your hands into the shot but have the intention of smashing the ball with a right-hand uppercut your hands will work exactly as they should. The back of your left hand and the palm of your right hand, in perfect "togetherness," will bring the clubface, going at top speed, correctly against the ball and keep it there, compressed, for that all-important fraction of a second that tells the story of direction and distance of the shot.

The result of the stinging whip of the ball was a 210-yard drive, much better than Bill expected, and mighty good for a better golfer than Bill, hitting into the wind.

"Partner, I'm proud of you. All your bubble-brained shots are forgiven. Please tell people you know me," I applauded Bill. I felt almost as good about the shot as he did.

Bill grinned and bowed.

He said, "Tommy, I've learned something I'll never forget. It is in my head indelibly. You weren't supposed to give any first aid this hole but you couldn't stand reading my mind. I had in the back of my head the impulse to hit the ball so hard I'd flatten it. When you stopped me you saved me from battering myself instead of the ball. I've always had the notion of hitting with Goliath's might instead of David's precision."

"Hallelujah, brother," I responded.

When we got to Bill's drive it was far enough down the fairway to give him the unique problem of keeping his second shot short of the cross-bunkering.

The bunkers were so far ahead there was only a remote chance of carrying them with another shot hit nearly as well as the drive Bill had just made. But still there was a temptation to try, so a fellow could say in the locker room later, "My second flew over the cross bunkers on the ninth."

Bill shoved Satan behind him and hit a graceful, unforced shot with a 4-wood. The brainwashing I'd given him about dismissing the impulse to hit hard had worked. The ball went like an arrow straight down the fairway and stopped in front of the trap.

With 140 yards to go, Bill took out a 7-iron. I knew he would pick the wrong club. He'd been surprising himself with more distance than he was accustomed to getting and he didn't judge this shot correctly. I could hardly blame him; he was in a location that was new to him after two shots.

Under normal conditions, a good lie and no wind, a 7-iron in the hands of an average golfer is good for 120 to 130 yards. With a breeze fluttering the flag toward us, Bill's 7-iron definitely wasn't the club to use. It would cost him one of the several strokes with which the average golfer penalizes himself every round by thoughtless choice of clubs.

Bill played the shot beautifully for him. It wasn't a shot to excite Hogan or Snead or to arouse the envy of Palmer, Finsterwald or Venturi but, outside of there not being enough of it, it was a Class-A shot.

He had a bit of luck, too. His ball must have hit a hard spot. It took a big bounce, then kept hopping toward the green.

The fairway to the apron of the green was level and the grass was mowed to short fairway length. A bit closer to the green and a putter would have been the approach club for Bill. I was afraid he was going to use his putter as he hauled it out of his bag. Then he took another look at the short stretch of fairway between his ball and the green and decided that the turf was a little too long for rolling the ball.

He gave his putter to his caddie and took out a 6-iron. I sighed in relief.

At this stage I was more apprehensive than Bill. Maybe Bill wasn't bothered at all. I hoped not. I was wondering if I'd told him, somewhere along the line, a peculiar thing about these delicate short shots: The grip must be firmer than on the other shots. There's no lash to these shots but a short, firm, precise smack, delivered smoothly.

Bill took an open stance with the ball off his right toe. His hands were close to his body. His right elbow was close to his ribs. His head was almost over the ball. He held the club at the lower part of the grip.

Bill made a short backswing. There was only a fraction of a break in his wrists. He hit the ball crisply, and when he finally turned his head to look at the shot with his left eye the ball was rolling straight for the pin. It was the only thing the ball could do. It had been hit neatly and crisply, like a long putt, with a club with some loft to it, and it had to shoot through the air in a low arc until it hit the green, then, with its overspin, roll along the line to the hole.

He had a six-inch putt for his par 5. 1 holed a tricky six-footer for mine.

All that was needed after Bill's feat of playing the hardest hole on the course the easy way, by using his head, was for him to ask me if there was any help he could give me with my game.

I was weak from the prolonged anxiety of Bill's conquest of the ninth and from the ordeals of the previous holes. I needed

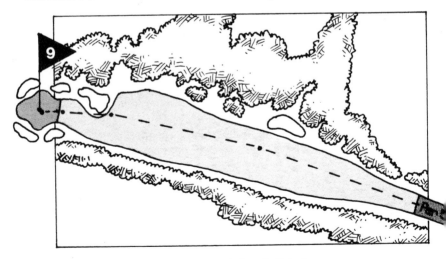

How Bill played the ninth hole

a drink of good, wholesome liquor to restore myself to my natural relaxed and untroubled state. I looked at the club-house and my nostrils quivered as a door opened and I got a sniff of the invigorating air that curled out from the grillroom.

"How about a slight detour for a dipper of internal lini-ment?" I suggested, and quickened my pace toward the club's life-saving station.

MEDITATIONS OF A GOLFER WHO IS ABOUT TO HAVE A DRINK

*A*s we walked toward the clubhouse Bill was exultant and bouncing. Reaction to the exertion of thinking at golf hadn't hit him yet.

I was tired but jubilant, too, at having performed a minor miracle — with the help of a golf ball and clubs I had brightened a man's future.

A discouraged and hopeless fellow who was quitting golf had been brought back to share in the delights of golf's companionship, to let his eyes dwell upon the loveliness of the countryside, to walk with exhilaration on the springy turf, swinging his arms and stretching his body. Bill knew now the joy of escape from the rat race. He could lift his chin because he had proved to himself that he was his own master. All those riches and more that golf gives were saved for a man who needs what golf has to give.

That's a good day's work for anybody.

The score is important, of course. And the discovery that you are superior to another golfer is satisfying. But when your score is bad and the other fellow beats you, golf still has been a blessing to you. The score isn't the "be all and end all."

You play the game by the rules and that in itself is an infallible mark of a gentleman of quality. Nobody ever cheats anybody else at golf. The one who is cheated is the one who cheats.

You keep your own score and you know what you have lost or won.

Golf has done wondrously well by me. My responsibility is to do as well as I can by golf. Helping Bill gave me an opportunity to make a payment on the debt I owe golf.

The day before I'd played with Bill, Ed and Jim and I had played a round with one of the brilliant youngsters of the tournament circuit who was confused and despondent. Fortunately, I was able to put my finger on the source of his slump and get him doing well again.

As in so many other cases the remedy was simple. The combination and coordination of factors involved in making a golf shot are so complex that people are inclined to look for something concealed and mysterious as a golf fault. The trouble generally is some simple little error that can be logically and quickly located and easily corrected.

In good golf there are only four fundamentals and you should keep reminding yourself of them. They are:

(1) a good grip of the club,
(2) a proper stance,
(3) good footwork,
(4) control and application of power.

That fourth fundamental, which is as important as the other points, requires swinging the club back and down in the groove with left-hand control and hitting with the right hand.

That is all there is to top-class mechanical golf. Although it doesn't seem like much, there can be thousands of hours of blood, sweat and tired muscles spent in converting those details into a perfect shot.

The ball, which can't read a line of all this, is lying there absolutely indifferent to being hit. You are the one with the problem. You've got to guide the club into the groove that leads to the ball and you can't guide and hit with the same hand.

Once you've lost control of the club you are entirely lost. Golf is not a game of smash and slug. Being big and strong doesn't give you an advantage in golf. Some little golfers have been tremendously long hitters. You can name Ben Hogan, Bobby Cruickshank and Bob Toski in that class of the little and long. It is the speed of the clubhead, not the size of the muscle, that accounts for the big distance shots in golf.

Because size and strength aren't paramount in golf you wonder why women don't show better in comparison with men's scoring. Women golfers, I think, work harder and concentrate in some departments of the game more than men. But the all-consuming desire for length defeats them. They haven't the type of frame and muscle for whipping the clubhead into the ball as fast as the proficient men can do it.

Women don't control their long or short shots as well as men. The short-game inferiority of good women golfers as rated by men's golf standards seems to be due to failure to devote as much studious practice to this department as men give it.

A short game as good as that of Paul Runyan's, when he was champion, would make any one of a half dozen of today's women professionals the greatest woman player in the game's history. There are several of the woman experts who are bigger and stronger than Paul was and hit longer than he did when he was defeating such powerful giants as Sam Snead, Craig Wood, Mortie Dutra, Henry Picard, Willie Goggin and Jimmy Hines.

Paul still controls wooden shots marvelously well. He taught a lot of noted professionals impressive lessons about control. When he shot first to the green and was on (as he generally was) he had a psychological advantage over the other fellow whose drive was fifteen to fifty yards longer than Runyan's. It is frightening to see how narrow a green can get after the other fellow gets there.

Control is underlined in putting. If you make the first putt for $1,000 the other fellow is putting for nothing.

As big and as powerful as Harry Vardon was, his shots seldom displayed his power. He was a smart golfer — one of the very smartest the game has ever known. The big holes he could reach in two shots, but he didn't bang at them with full steam ahead unless he found it wisely necessary. At the first National Open in which I played in the United States — the one in 1920 at Inverness at Toledo — I remember Vardon being on the

Correct action on the backswing

Feet planted firmly, weight evenly distributed at address, the clubhead

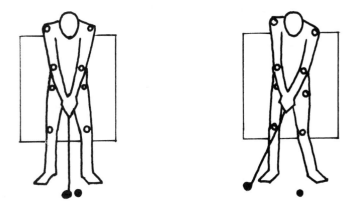

is swept back with the hands, mainly the left. Arms are extended until the elbows and wrists break naturally. Left knee begins to bend and

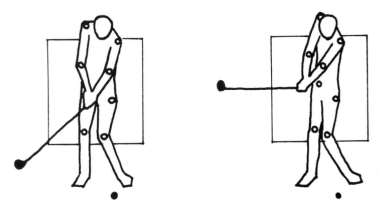

point toward ball as left heel lifts. Weight shifts gradually to right leg. Hips and shoulders rotate.

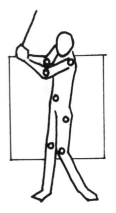
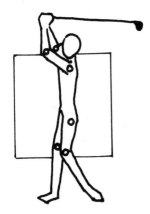

After a momentary pause, the downswing begins. The right knee

begins to come in toward the ball as the weight gradually shifts from right to left. The left hand maintains control as the hips and shoulders

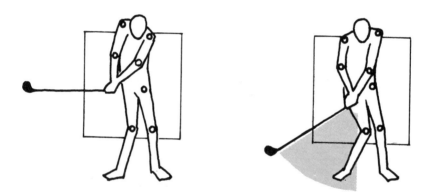

rotate in reverse to the backswing. Smoothness is the keynote until the right hand snaps in with the power (shaded sections).

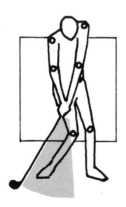
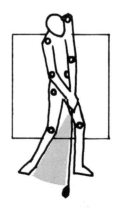

Up until the moment of impact, the hands have been ahead of the

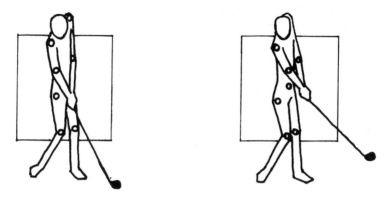

clubhead. Now, after the right hand has supplied the power and the
clubhead smacks the ball, keep the arms extended and let your hands

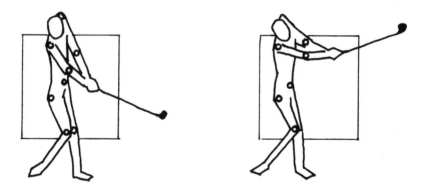

swing on and out naturally toward your target. Hips and shoulders ro-
tate to a smooth finish.

ninth green each round in two shots. The hole was about 470 yards long and had a narrow opening. Jim Barnes was a long hitter and was twenty-five yards ahead of Vardon in one round, I recall, but Vardon was on the green first.

Vardon could hit the ball harder and keep it straighter than anybody else I've ever seen. He could always bring forth that extra something that he needed to get more length, but he seldom had to call on it, he was so consistently precise.

Precision is a key word in golf but you don't see the average golfer trying to establish high precision in his game, practicing on shots that require accuracy rather than distance. If he does work on his short game he doesn't stay "average" long; he improves emphatically.

Precision starts with the control of the club by the fingers.

Then after getting dependable controlling grip of the club, the ordinary golfer doesn't pay enough attention to his stance. When the grip and the stance are neglected the chances of hitting the ball precisely are minimized. When due attention is given to these factors the chances of missing the shot are decidedly reduced.

Then, as I'd often noticed during the nine holes my three comrades and I had played, there is something else that prevents precise shotmaking — the common tendency to lurch and sway instead of standing still and using the hands to hit the ball.

I'd had several occasions to remind Bill that he was using his body like a blocking back in football instead of using it to put him in position to use his hands properly.

Often when most golfers think they are swinging they don't really turn the torso. They merely turn their shoulders. That's fine, but not enough. They've got to turn the hips also. You can't turn your hips without your shoulders turning.

While the body is being turned the head has to stay still as the hub of the rotating action. Head steadiness is a vital habit to be cultivated on the practice tee. If Bill hadn't been able to keep his head pretty well fixed as the center of his swing on most shots, I wouldn't have been able to do much for him as we played.

A great deal of the explanation of head steadiness — or lack of it — is as far away from the head as you can get. The answers are in your feet.

If your footwork is good your head will stay steady and you'll be able to turn around a stable axis.

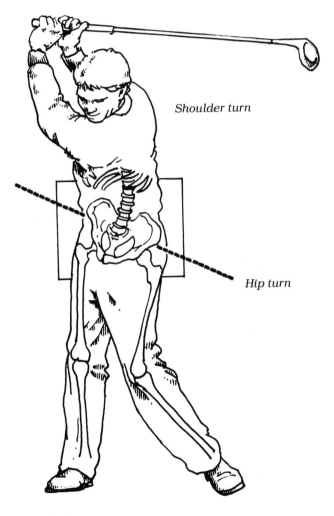

Shoulder turn

Hip turn

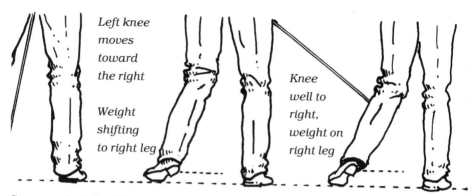

Left knee moves toward the right

Weight shifting to right leg

Knee well to right, weight on right leg

Stance — both feet flat

Correct footwork for full backswing

Footwork is enormously important in all sports of movement but I question if it is as important in any other game as it is in golf.

You've got to be flexible on your feet to get your knees and hips moving, to make it possible to swing properly.

The backswing starts imperceptibly in your left foot. In a full backswing your right foot stays on the ground and your weight is transferred until the right foot bears more of it than the left. The left foot is slightly lifted and the left knee is pointed to a spot well to the right of the ball. Footwork that shows the proper pointing of the left knee forces you to turn your hips correctly in the backswing. If you don't turn your hips it is impossible to get into the right position at the top of the swing.

Some younger players who are very limber and who don't mind risking back injuries that will shorten their careers restrict the left foot action, keeping the heel almost on the ground and twisting with the inside of the sole digging into the turf.

The short shots that require very little body action can be played almost flatfooted and with the left knee dipping a very

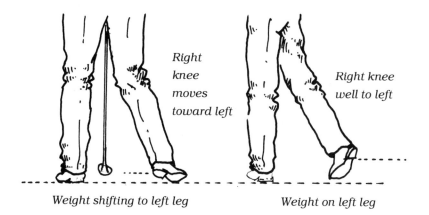

Right knee moves toward left

Right knee well to left

Weight shifting to left leg

Weight on left leg

Correct footwork for downswing

little bit, perhaps, toward the ball instead of turning to the right.

Keep your knees loose and your feet carrying your weight evenly distributed from toe to heel at address and you have a good foundation that will stay with you.

From that foundation you can build a perfect backswing.

At the top of the backswing the knees of the expert golfer are rather close together, and at the end of his swing his knees are even closer to each other. When the knees work that way the footwork is perfect. The knees of the 100-shooter are widely separated at the top of the backswing and at the finish.

It is certain that the first movement in the downswing is the left foot setting flat onto the ground and fixing the axis of the downswing. As the left foot comes down the excellent golfer almost simultaneously gets his right foot working. He pushes from his right big toe, and his right knee goes in toward his left knee.

Every golfer of Bill's type has heard talk that he only vaguely understood about "getting his left side out of the way." If his footwork is as it should be the push from his right foot will get his left side into a location where it can't block his swing, and his right side will bring his right hand into the ideal position for hitting with the right hand.

Good footwork is a primary requisite of fine golf. No substitute for the best in footwork, no subterfuge, can be permitted.

A couple of times I'd had to show Bill how his footwork was coordinated with his shoulder action. When the footwork was good the right shoulder was bound to come underneath the chin in a fine uppercutting movement instead of going around horizontally as Bill was disposed to swing when he got careless and operated in the duffer manner.

It is a series of delicate, exquisitely coordinated movements from the feet up that makes golf a great game. Your shot management starts in your head but your shotmaking starts in your feet.

So much for the technicalities. I've done so much thinking and applying thought in improving my game and the games of others that I habitually review any lesson right after I've concluded it. I've corrected errors of omission and commission in these introspective reviews and once in a while have learned something fresh — or a fresh way of presenting the old stuff.

And now, pardon me a moment: "Waiter, please refuel me."

As my request was attended to Bill sagged in his chair. He sighed, "Tommy, only nine holes and I never was so tired in my life."

I moistened my larynx. "That's the penalty you have to pay for unique labor with your head on that nine. After you have trained yourself to think at golf you will enjoy the game more and it will be less work for you."

"At that, I've never enjoyed nine holes more in my life," Bill said.

"That goes for me, too," Ed echoed. "I didn't have any idea there was so much more to golf than hitting the ball."

Jim stared at his empty glass as though he were looking at a crystal ball. He came out of his trance and remarked, "I've played a lot of golf and I've played a lot of other games. I've hunted and fished all over the whole damn world. But until I listened this afternoon I never had an idea how much fun and what self-examination a game could be."

"Maybe I didn't do you any good. You may feel ashamed of yourself when you play a stupid shot from here in," I replied.

"That's true, but think of how elated I will be when I out-brain a golf ball," Jim retorted.

Jim and Ed had been in on a pass in the arrangement I'd made to take Bill as a partner. I was glad to hear they'd benefited from being in the bleachers but I was concerned only with determining whether I'd accomplished anything with Bill.

After analyzing his performance and his score I decided that I had succeeded better than I had anticipated. In nine holes Bill had gained knowledge that is power and had got basic training in how to apply that learning. He had learned, I trusted, a great deal about how to simplify golf and that's a very tough subject to handle. His card was nothing wonderful- 5 8 3 5 6 4 3 5 5 = 44 — but even with that 8 on the second, it was strokes better than he'd been scoring for the nine. The way he was playing now, using his head as well as his muscles, I felt he had a good chance to crack 40 on the back nine.

The human being has an urge to complicate golf to such an extent that the only way the game could be played is with a huge battery of mechanical brains. Then when the complications don't work, the golfer is foggy about the cause of failure, fearful of shotmaking because of sand and water, and gets packed so tightly with details that he can't move. He struggles in panic, utterly without organizing his thought and action, without an informed, definite and constructive policy.

As I reflected on my experience with Bill I reached the conclusion that the best thing I'd done for Bill was to show him how to help himself. The test of my efforts for and with him would come when he was playing without me and he'd have to work out his own combination of mechanics and mentality.

Would he begin to survey the situation, determine a plan, then play with reason? Or would he backslide to the original sin of the duffer — totter stiffly at the shot, take a swing that would be too long or too jerky and short, have every muscle as stiff as a wire, and throw his body at the ball?

I concluded that I'd done right by Bill. I'd tried to get inside his mind and it hadn't been as difficult as I had expected it might be.

He showed signs of learning the very hard job of hitting the ball easily. He didn't realize that he had passed a revealing test on that point when he played the ninth. He was a bit tired and in that condition fatigue pushes a fellow into trying to hit harder, when he should keep his body steady and hit easier but faster with his hands.

Bill hadn't conquered his golf problems or learned any multimillion-dollar "secret," but he had found out how to use what he did know about golf. He was in a position to teach himself a lot more, and to absorb from competent professionals more of what they endeavor to get him to learn.

After the third quick application of pain-killer I began to think there might have been so much progress made in nine holes that Bill would expect perfection from now on. He and the other fellows were starting to talk profoundly about the game. Every golfer is an expert in the club's grillroom.

"Don't get too good at it all of a sudden," I warned. "You may be like the 100-shooter who met his pals on the far shore of the Styx. The yarn must have been old when Old Tom Morris was a babe; all golf stories were. But here it is:

"The deceased exchanged merry greetings, then one of the recent arrivals asked the 100-shooter, 'Get in any golf here?'

"The 100-shooter said, 'Uh-huh, every day. Wonderful course. And I am great! But something happened to me after I left you guys. I did a 60 the first time I played this course and every day I get 30 going out and 30 coming in for my 60 on a course that makes Pine Valley look easy.'

"'Sixty every round?' asked one of the late lamented. 'I thought heaven would be more exciting.'"

"The 100-shooter looked scornfully at the speaker. He said, 'What the hell, you are in hell!'"

After respectful laughter at that item of golfers' folklore, Bill gave marching orders. "Come on, boys, let's get at the back nine."

My three comrades got up from their chairs. I stayed sitting.

"Go to it, fellows, and good luck. I've just played 900 holes — 9 outside and 891 inside my skull. I am tired. Include me out. Thanks for a pleasant game. And for your money, too, when you get around to paying Bill and me."

"Think nothing of it," said Ed, smiling. "Sorry you're not coming along to see what happens when we are all on our own."

"I'll do all right, Tommy, and a few million thanks to you," Bill told me as the three left for the tenth tee.

And, as an elegy might put it, the golfers outward plod their eager ways and leave the world to the waiter, the bartender, and me.